I0418457

Highly Favored?

Discovering Hope in the Shadows of Grief

by Denette Schaer

Copyright © 2024 Denette Schaer

All rights reserved. No part of this publication may be reproduced, distributed, or transmitted in any form or by any means, including photocopying, recording, or other electronic or mechanical methods, without the prior written permission of the publisher, except in the case of brief quotations embodied in critical reviews and certain other noncommercial uses permitted by copyright law.

Scripture quotations are taken from the Holy Bible, New International Version®, NIV®. Copyright © 1973, 1978, 1984, 2011 by Biblica, Inc.™ Used by permission of Zondervan. All rights reserved worldwide. www.zondervan.comThe "NIV" and "New International Version" are trademarks registered in the United States Patent and Trademark Office by Biblica, Inc.™

ISBN: 979-8-9887256-2-6 (Paperback)
ISBN: 979-8-9887256-3-3 (Hardcover)
ISBN: 979-8-9887256-4-0 (eBook)

Editing by Abbey McLaughlin
Cover Design by Jillian Dutch

Acknowledgements

To my husband, my best friend: This journey has been done together, and there is no one else I could have ever seen myself doing it with. Thank you for being our rock and for leading us so well during our hardest season. You are truly the same person behind closed doors, and I am forever grateful I chose you.

To my sons, Dylan and Nathan: You are forever and always will be my greatest calling and reward. I am forever proud of you both. Your strength amazes me. Keep taking the next right step. I love you forever and like you for always.

To Emmeline and Corinne: Thank you for how you have loved my boys and our family. You have been fierce protectors and loved well through it all. You both are and forever will be two of my biggest answers to prayer this side of heaven.

To my dirt sitters (you know who you are): I really don't know if our family would have made it without you and the overwhelming grace you loved our family with during our darkest days. Thank you for not giving up on us.

Highly Favored?

Discovering Hope in the Shadows of Grief

by Denette Schaer

Table of Contents

Introduction

Growing up, I was taught that God's favor meant blessings and yellow brick roads. For most of my life, that was true. And then, one late-spring evening, all my notions of the way God treats us and cares for us came crumbling down. I lost my son in a car accident; he was only seventeen. Suddenly, the God I had in my head didn't match the one I was talking to, crying to, and questioning. It has taken all the pain, tears, counseling, lament, and heartache I have in my weary body to wrestle with this new understanding of God, but as I do, I've wanted to share it with others. With shaky faith, I am doing my best to declare the things I know about God to be true regardless of the circumstances life has thrown at us.

May 30, 2022 was the hardest and worst day of my entire life. A dramatic way to start a book titled *Highly Favored*, I know, but that is exactly what it was, and I hope that reality will never be contested. I want you to know that if you find yourself in a season of confusion and doubt, you are not alone. It's okay to wonder who God is after so long thinking you knew.

It's hard to feel "favored" in these seasons. It seems like a contradiction to say we're favored by God while walking through hell. Favor may seem so far from where life has brought you, and hearing others use that word can make you sick to your stomach. Trust me. I understand. One day, I may have more poetic phrases or holy words of understanding worthy enough to be penned to paper, but for now, I am faced with the insurmountable weight that sometimes we will walk through things we will never fully understand on this side of heaven, and it does not mean I am not loved and seen fully by God.

This is my attempt at holy lament. Some days, maybe we look like Precious Moments dolls, our hands folded and sitting politely on our knees. But a lot of days, holy lament looks like pacing, weeping, and salivating like a rabid dog vulnerably in front of God. As I walk out my pain and my grief, I am (not for the first time but assuredly in the grandest way) being forced to look at what I truly believe about the God I have served since I was five years old. I am being forced to look at the power of His promises in light of a hurting and broken world.

The Bible says, "His mercies are new every morning," but what does that mean for the one like me that was scared of a new day? (Lamentations 3:22-23) The one scared for the sun to come up because it meant the nightmare from the night before is their actual reality? Cliché phrases, nice platitudes, and even "highly favored" Bible verses can feel like salt in the wound when walking through despair.

"God only takes the good ones."

"Everything happens for a reason!"

"God makes all things work together for good."

The most frustrating platitude I've been given in the past couple years has been that this loss is a sign of God's favor in my life. That because I've been tasked with the impossible weight of loss, God must have big plans for me. That gave no kind of hope to my aching and heartbroken soul. I had lost my *son* after all. My youngest of three amazing boys at the age of seventeen, and his wonderful girlfriend, lost their lives in a horrific and tragic way. In the months that have followed, fully consumed by my own tears and waves of sorrow, the phrase "highly favored" seems to continue to make its way into my arguments with God and continues to echo in what feels like emptiness. Highly favored? *Really God?* Highly favored? What does that even mean?

I think twenty journals have been given to me in the past few months. People keep telling me I have a story to share, and I guess the best way for them to show encouragement is evident by the stack of empty journals that have shown up in care baskets or our mailbox or at the front door. They now tower beside my bedside table, almost taunting me to be truthful and honest about what is really in my heart.

Truth be told, I know God asked me to start writing years ago. Call it insecurity, disobedience, or fear, but I never have had the courage to put pen to paper (or fingers to keys). I truly feel like there may be multiple books stuck deep inside my bones. Not because I am so smart, want to be heard, or even have a lot to say, but because I feel like what I'm learning (even in spite of my pain and on really dark days) is too good to keep to myself and maybe someone else needs to hear it as well.

I hope that someone is you. I hope that together, as we dig into that phrase "highly favored," we can hash it out with God. I won't pretend to have all the answers (as I'm assuming you don't either). I only intend to start a real, raw, and authentic conversation that not only looks into the face of favor as some victorious medal of honor, but one with a great price and weight attached to it. A conversation on a title that had I honestly been given the chance to choose or not to choose, I would have picked the latter every time. I want to be so bold to dig into the stories a little more, peel back the promises and the provision, in order to see just how much the sacrifice of a highly favored life may cost.

I also want to take a good hard look at the people God called his "favored ones" and the reality that most, if given the chance, would have never chosen it. You see most times when we think of favor, we only think of the mountaintop experiences. The ones who made it. The ones picked first for the team and the ones who have it all.

I am enamored embarrassingly enough by what I like to call "trash TV" and can binge a good Netflix show with the best of them. I can waste a good day watching the lifestyles of the rich and famous or families jet-setting across the world (even though my ideal day of fun is actually getting a great deal at the local thrift store). Why do I like watching stories based on realities I'll most likely never have? Because their lives feel like a dream. In the comforts of my living room couch, tucked under my cozy blanket, their yacht-setting adventures and star-studded clinking toasts feel like favor. It feels like they are the ones we should be striving to be, but is that what God meant by the term? When He used the word "favor," was He picturing the stories of first-world success shared by the influencers we follow on social media (many times covered with filters or fillers) or is there more? Maybe our lives, our war-torn lives filled with lack and broken hearts, are more closely aligned with those He called "highly favored." I know what you are thinking (at least I know what I'm thinking). I'm not sure I want to sign up for what You are dishing out, Lord. Honestly, I wouldn't even want the cars and the clothes, but at least my family all together, happy and whole. What I'm hoping we will both see as we turn these pages and I do my best to type with weary fingers, and a heavy heart and soul is that His picture is much bigger than at first glance and even possibly more beautiful.

Easy? No.

Desired? Maybe not.

Marketable? In no single way.

But more beautiful? I surely hope so.

Please take it from a mother's heart that is breaking while walking, He bears our pain and repurposes it, and even though it may not be what we want (or even what we have prayed), He is there to show us how to make it through, one breath at a time.

Chapter 1

Favor Ain't Fair

Have you ever heard the term "favor ain't fair"? If not, no worries. It's a term thrown around in a lot of Christian circles, and I should know. I've been in enough circles to make me dizzy. Sometimes the phrase is used in serious tones, and other times, it's thrown around as a joke. "Favor Ain't Fair" is like the tagline, "Only God could coordinate this!" or "God's looking out for me!" In my life, it's been used jovially for times we *benefit* from favor.

You get the front parking spot on a dreaded busy day at Walmart? *Favor ain't fair!* Lord must be watching out for us!

You get picked by a friend that has a big bank account or fancy title to go to some fancy event, and you even get to cut everyone else standing in line for front-row seats! *Favor ain't fair!* Sometimes God just loves on His children like that.

The cashier rings you up and the item is fifty percent cheaper than you thought it would be because it was on sale. You guessed it: *"favor ain't fair!"*

My family and I had gotten pretty used to the term. We threw it around like a hot potato, never once considering it could potentially burn or sting one day as we heard it used by others. If I'm honest, the phrase can now make my stomach turn, especially in church contexts like sermons and books.

My husband and I have been in ministry for over seventeen years now. As a pastor's wife with three growing boys, I could tell you about miracle upon miracle we have witnessed in our lives up to this point. Many we would have measured by that "favor ain't fair" mentality—("God must just love us!"). We had to and we needed to. Some seasons when we were "doing the Lord's work" (it's more fun if you say it with a southern drawl), we had so little that without God, we would've gone without. We have had so many leaps of faith, and yet we saw God catch us each and every time. We also saw God provide when maybe those we were serving or serving with didn't see the value in us. Often when starting out in ministry, you don't get paid very well, if at all. I'll never forget when my husband gave his heart to Jesus and felt called into ministry. Our testimony is a crazy one and maybe another topic for another time, but I was so excited for his newfound love to share Jesus with others that I wasn't concerned about how God would meet our needs.

His first ministry job, we truly had to stand fast on the hopes that we would see a reward one day in heaven because the $100 a week they were able to pay him to run an inner-city sports ministry wasn't going to feed three hungry and growing boys. To be honest, we didn't care. Why? Because God always supplied our needs. We constantly saw Him come through. We had gift cards dropped off at our house anonymously the one Christmas I cried out to God because we couldn't afford gifts. We had food dropped off by dear friends who had taken a look at our barren fridge and knew our boys were sick of peanut butter and jelly and Triangle-o's (those are the discount store brand of Doritos, just in case you were wondering). When we were told our minivan was about to exhale its final breath and wasn't worth the new engine, we saw God provide a new car (well not new, but new to us) as a *gift*, and then we saw God do it again when we needed another vehicle. We were like a family at Oprah's "Twelve Days of Christmas" for used cars. We even saw God miraculously heal our son. We all saw it. Our kids saw it. Our friends saw it, and we all declared it.

Favor ain't fair.

We saw God so many times, especially in those first years of truly laying it all down to pursue Him that maybe somewhere along the way, *my heart began to believe that the goodness of God is equated with the provision of God.* I began to bury deep in my heart that as long as I was a "good" girl and did all the things I was supposed to, not only would all my needs be met but also my fears kept at bay. I was fervently ignoring Matthew 5:45:

> *He causes his sun to rise on the evil and the good, and sends rain on the righteous and the unrighteous.*

The just and the unjust. I have been both, truly. I think we all have, but what I realize now as I sit here and attempt to share my heart with you is that I had gotten so used to seeing favor as miracles on miracles (a million little miracles) that I never once was brave enough to wonder why He answers "yes" for some and "no" for others. Looking into the faces of those chasing God, even those I loved and those I was called to minister to, who were hurting and struggling with really hard and dark things, I've had to realize *His favor not only* can *be in both the good and the bad, but* is *in both!* Both the mountain and the pit. Both the win and the loss. Both the birth of something new and the death of what we thought would be.

Until months ago (as a self-declared empath), I would be very guarded about how much darkness and sadness I would let my eyes gaze at. I tend to pick up people's hurts and add them to my own heavy bag of feelings, so I was careful how much loss or hurt I would even allow myself to experience. There can be wisdom in not picking up others' hurts or offenses, but there can also be negligence in not helping someone else out of the pit (anyone remember the story of the Good Samaritan?). I can now say that although it wasn't my intention, in the name of self-preservation, I would often turn my eyes away from those hurting too much in an attempt to protect myself from the pain. What I'm now realizing is that God can give me the strength to climb into someone else's pit or at the least (and I do mean the very least) let them know they are seen and not alone.

"Today we are going to wash your hair."

I'll always remember when Mollie said that to me. It was my first step not away from grief but alongside it, leaning on someone else's strength. Our dear friends Mollie and Tito had come running at the first sound of the loss of our son and took up camp in our home for a few weeks. They decided to do more than just say they were praying for us; they showed up and much like Job's friends, decided to sit in the dirt with us. I can only imagine how much my stench must have rivaled Job's as my dear friend decided to not only encourage me but tell me, "Today we are going to wash your hair."

I had not left my spot on the couch. I had sunk deep into despair after getting home with one less child. I was growing a pretty gnarly dreadlock and hadn't even changed clothes in the days after the accident. I could barely eat, and I did nothing but look at the large canvas hanging directly over me that showed the three beautiful smiles of my three happy and whole children.

I contested her offer and sincere attempt at helping me with the wails more often heard out of a toddler. She looked at me and said, "You either go in by yourself, or I get naked with you!" She was so determined to remind me that I was not alone, she was going to *prove* it. She was walking out God-sized strength for a friend who needed a glimpse of it.

His strength goes where we go. Even if we don't feel it. Even if we need to be reminded of it. We don't leave His strength on the mountaintop. He goes where I go, and I take His strength with me. In the beginning of Jesus' Sermon on the Mount, His teaching starts with beatitudes. It means "blessings." He starts His sermon to the huge crowd by "blessing" them.

> *Now when Jesus saw the crowds, he went up on a mountainside and sat down. His disciples came to him, and he began to teach them.*
>
> *He said:*
>
> *"Blessed are the poor in spirit,*
>
> > *for theirs is the kingdom of heaven.*
>
> *"Blessed are those who mourn,*
>
> > *for they will be comforted.*
>
> *"Blessed are the meek,*
>
> > *for they will inherit the earth.*
>
> *"Blessed are those who hunger and thirst for righteousness,*
>
> > *for they will be filled.*
>
> *"Blessed are the merciful,*
>
> > *for they will be shown mercy.*

"Blessed are the pure in heart,

 for they will see God.

"Blessed are the peacemakers,

 for they will be called children of God.

"Blessed are those who are persecuted because of righteousness,

 for theirs is the kingdom of heaven.

"Blessed are you when people insult you, persecute you and falsely say all kinds of evil against you because of me."

(Matthew 5:1-11)

Do those sound like blessings to you? Maybe some of them sound amazing, like the merciful and pure-in-heart blessings. I'll take those any day, but the others...I don't want to be poor in anything, but especially in spirit...yet here I am.

Those who mourn? I'm yet to graduate from crying every day. More days than not, buckets of tears.

Meek (which the world sees as "weak")?

Peacemakers (which means there's strife and messy people to deal with)?

Persecuted and reviled?

Sometimes I wonder if Jesus was blessing them or cursing them. These are the real conversations that I have with God these late nights. As regular humans in moments of suffering, it's hard to read your blessings, Jesus, and walk away stronger in who we are called to be and in who You truly are. If nothing is wasted—which is what I truly with all the fight left in me and with all my resolve choose to believe (sometimes with clenched fists and a quivering lip)—how on earth do I reconcile mourning, hunger, meekness, and persecution as a *blessing?*

C.S. Lewis says so eloquently, "God whispers to us in our pleasure, speaks in our conscience, but shouts in our pain." I can't speak for you or your hurts and hang-ups, but I do know this about myself: I love the pleasures in this life. I love the happy times with family, the parties and the parades. I have lived a life trying to make the most of every moment. One of my greatest rewards and treasures has been the days, hours, or just *minutes* we have lived life to the fullest as a family. I love the lights and all the yummy foods of each and every holiday and celebration, and I don't think there is anything wrong with that. He grants us those amazing gifts in this life.

I can also tell you that I have never, not once, been pressed to grapple with God's character and faithfulness during the great times. You just don't wonder if God's good while He's blessing you. I have cherished great times for sure, but never been *forced* to grow through them. No. For me, it has always been in the dark days. When I have had to truly dig myself up out of the pit and make a choice to keep standing. Those are the days that I have seen breakthroughs. Those are the days I have had to seek the face of God. What would I need a breakthrough from if I was never stuck in despair?

Maybe the beatitudes are our glimpse into the hurt that God sees every time He looks at this broken world. It's our moment to understand that yes, the world is a hurting world, but we are also supposed to do something about it.

Blessed are those who mourn? I will never be able to look at a mother losing or who has lost a child the same way ever again. I was given a glimpse of what it looks like. I was allowed to see what that loss truly means. It does not feel like a blessing.

Blessed are the peacemakers? I wish my story of being a pastor's wife was filled with love notes and roses every Sunday, but instead, it was more filled with picking up students from places they needed rescuing, wiping snotty noses in kids church, and praying for someone we were called to love on that was actually cursing my own family behind closed doors. I can only for a moment, in my small-minded self, try to feel what Jesus must have felt when He came to this aging and rotting planet to love on a people He sacrificed even unto death, only to be cursed.

When we walk through our trials, we are given real-time access to how He sees things. In seeing the hurting, He gives us a glimpse of what should have never been—a broken world—and reveals what should truly be: a life with Him. A piece of heaven. He trusts us to see it as He sees it when He trusts us to carry heavy things because He knows firsthand that how you walk with the broken is more important than how you sit with the great.

When my boys were each thirteen years of age, God had laid on my heart so heavily to take them (just mom and son) on their very first mission trip. These trips will forever be ingrained in my heart as some of the most precious moments with each of my boys. I wanted them, as they navigated what life looked like as a teen, to realize and see the world as much bigger than the life they had built around them. I wanted them to catch a glimpse of the world as God sees it. God was so faithful to have seemingly handpicked each trip for each boy.

My oldest and I traveled for thirty-three hours and went to the Amazon, down river, for ten days. We were completely cut off from the world as we slept in hammocks on the Amazon River and ministered to villages that could only be seen at certain times of the year when the water was high enough for the large boat to gain access to them. Talk about having to come out of your comfort zone! My oldest, who loved his little box of comfort, was kicked so far out of it that he actually loved his new sleeping arrangement and brought a hammock back home and slept in it for eighteen months in his own bedroom.

My middle son and I traveled to Tegucigalpa (Honduras), where we visited inner-city schools and shared the gospel in some of the most at-risk neighborhoods in not only the city but the world. Little did I know this was one of the most dangerous cities at the time. I signed up for the trip not realizing we would be welcomed with automatic weapons at pretty much every stop. Nor did I know that he would be mobbed (literally *mobbed*) by girls who thought he was Justin Bieber's younger brother all because of his long blonde "Shreveport Swoop" haircut.

My youngest son and I had the privilege to go to Haiti. In all my travels (by myself and with my sons), my heart had never ached so much. The level of hardship, hunger, and darkness was palpable. It was and to date the most spiritually dark and heaviest place I have ever traveled. I met mothers who had lost children. I met mothers who had given their children up for adoption not because they didn't love them or want them but simply because they could not feed them. I met mothers who had to decide which child they would keep over which child they could not. My heart couldn't imagine the pain they had to endure, and honestly, I didn't want to imagine.

I now look back at those trips I took with my sons, especially the last trip, and realize that I had no idea how to love and minister to those mothers because I had not been given what they had been given. Mourning.

Now I see it. Now I know the feeling. Do I want it? No. Do I want to understand it? No. But I've been given a glimpse of something that only someone who lives through it can comprehend. I did my best to love on those mamas while they were carrying loss or the weight and fear of the unknown of their children's future. I never once considered their child may in actuality outlive mine and there would be no third-year visit watching him play soccer with his newfound friends that came running to meet him that second year. Only someone that has been given the opportunity to carry something can truly know the weight of it.

Why is something so beautiful sent after we lose someone? Flowers, flowers, and more flowers showed up to our door those first few days and weeks. Everyone grieves differently, so please hear my heart if you are reading this and happened to send us flowers unknowingly or have sent flowers to someone as a sign of love. I know most people who receive a beautiful bouquet of flowers love the sentiment, but I was outraged as the doorbell would ring with delivery after delivery. My youngest son had always picked flowers for me. I have picture after picture and memories from everywhere of him handpicking me flowers. (Sometimes in places he assuredly wasn't supposed to. Sorry Disney World and to our local Publix florists).

Just two weeks before God welcomed him home, as we walked up to our local gym to work out together, he picked me a flower from in front of the Planet Fitness and said "remember when I used to always pick you flowers as a little boy? I always will."

So you can imagine my heartache as one bouquet after another appeared on my doorstep. Please forgive me, but at one point, I got so angry at what I know was people's attempt at love that I shouted assuredly loud enough for our neighbors to wonder why, "No more fucking flowers!"

I was so angry that what many meant to bring me cheer and hope was actually a stunning reminder of my loss. Crazy enough, the only thing I can now buy for my son and bring to honor the place his physical body now rests is a new bouquet of flowers. Knowingly more so for my heart than for his.

The void between God's promises and loss can sometimes be so overwhelmingly gaping that seeing hope (even in the cross) can feel unattainable. When we look to a Savior that we know is the perfect Son of God, it can feel as though even He can't understand the pain we are walking through. After all, we aren't perfect like Him. But I am learning in my darkest moment that there are so many parts of Jesus I never knew. Facets of Him that I never took the time (or desired) to know and understand.

He is not just a healer and a redeemer. He is the tempted and the tried. Bearing God's favor meant saying "No" to the devil one-on-one for forty days in a desert. Because God favored Jesus, Pharisees hovered around him like bees on a barbecue plate. He is not just a provider and sanctifier. He is the betrayed and forsaken. The same people who cheered His name yelled to crucify Him the next—and Jesus was asked to obey the Father and therefore the people's decision. That doesn't mean it wasn't frustrating and painful and confusing.

One of the most powerful things Jesus ever uttered was, *"My God, my God, why have you forsaken me?"* (Matthew 27:46). If Jesus struggled with feeling forsaken by God, why do we shake our heads in disbelief or annoyance when we ourselves or others struggle with the same feelings? Jesus did not deny the feelings He had as He hung there on that cross. He did not pray away the pain or deny the weight of it. He felt. He wept. He hurt *and* He prayed. Through all the suffering and loss, through all the heartache and grief and betrayal, He still called out *to* heaven and *to* His Father. The weight of favor was the ability to hold both promises and pain in the same weary body. Perhaps His strength came from the privilege of knowing God so intimately, of existing within the eternal safety of God's presence before he was born on earth, and from seeing how God delivered His promises from a bird's-eye view so many times before. He experienced the promises of heaven, so he carried the weight of the world to ensure you and I would too.

I don't think any other human could bear what Jesus did as gracefully as He did. God chose Jesus' favor very intentionally. We need to be cautious when we beg God for favor. The weight of it may be more than we bargained for.

Man of Sorrows

"Man of Sorrows," what a name
For the Son of God who came
Ruined sinners to reclaim!

Hallelujah! What a Savior!
Bearing shame and scoffing rude,
In my place condemned He stood;
Sealed my pardon with His blood;

Hallelujah! What a Savior!
Guilty, vile, and helpless, we,
Spotless Lamb of God was He;
Full redemption – can it be?

Hallelujah! What a Savior!
Lifted up was He to die,
"It is finished!" was His cry;
Now in heaven exalted high;

Hallelujah! What a Savior!
When He comes, our glorious King,
To His kingdom us to bring,
Then anew this song we'll sing
Hallelujah! What a Savior!

Chapter 2

Long-Suffering God

I have really struggled within the walls of the church this past year. Songs that used to encourage my heart now sting and cause tears. I am tired of first-world theology—the kind that teaches faith as a correlation with blessing and protection, as though the more we believe, the less suffering we might endure. How can that be when Jesus endured everything? Jesus was the *most* faith-full. His suffering was certainly not for lack of faith. In fact, highly favored, faith-full people in the Bible suffered quite a bit.

Teaching a belief system that praying hard enough, being good enough, or having "more" faith is the measuring stick to answered prayer would have never given room or allowed Jesus' death on a cross. If belief and obedience are the catalyst for a life of less suffering, surely that cup would have passed over Him. His will would have been exactly that of the Father's. No. If our way of understanding God and the gospel can't withstand the darkness of the shadows of Auschwitz, then it doesn't stand (a paraphrase of Viktor Frankl). If our Sunday sermons don't speak to those on the mountaintop *and* in the valley, are they helping or hurting?

Rather than disregarding the hurting people, rather than labeling them "ye of little faith," Jesus paid loving attention to them. Jesus stopped what he was doing for them. Jesus preached to them. The heart of this loving Savior is revealed over and over again in the gospels, and one of my all-time favorite parables (or stories) He shared is that of the Good Samaritan.

> *In reply Jesus said: "A man was going down from Jerusalem to Jericho, when he was attacked by robbers. They stripped him of his clothes, beat him and went away, leaving him half dead. A priest happened to be going down the same road, and when he saw the man, he passed by on the other side. So too, a Levite, when he came to the place and saw him, passed by on the other side. But a Samaritan, as he traveled, came where the man was; and when he saw him, he took pity on him. He went to him and bandaged his wounds, pouring on oil and wine. Then he put the man on his own donkey, brought him to an inn and took care of him. The next day he took out two denarii and gave them to the innkeeper. 'Look after him,' he said, 'and when I return, I will reimburse you for any extra expense you may have.'*
>
> *"Which of these three do you think was a neighbor to the man who fell into the hands of robbers?"*
>
> *The expert in the law replied, "The one who had mercy on him."*
>
> *Jesus told him, "Go and do likewise."*

(Luke 10:30-37)

This story reveals so much about the heart of this Jesus, I'm learning new pieces of every day. He's not disgusted with our wounds. He doesn't turn away from our despair; He runs towards it. This picture of the Samaritan spits in the face of racism and religion. He wasn't concerned about the titles of the men who passed the hurting, or even why they were in such a hurry to get on about their day. He was consumed with the heart of the man that took the time to see the hurting and stooped low to help another, regardless of what that man could do for him in return.

The same Jesus who flipped tables in the temple in the face of the religious also washed the feet of fisherman. Social constructs, boundaries, or expectations didn't stop Him from treating everyone with equal love. The angriest He ever got was with the religious elite, not the desperate and needy. I want to see the wounded not as an assignment or a detour but as He sees them: priceless. He isn't rushing me to the redemption before sitting with me while I'm knocked down. He sees my wounds and blesses them. He allows us to heal not to hide our scars but show others (as He has) that they reveal purpose.

My God isn't just a suffering God, but a long-suffering God. He knows it well. His promises are "yes and amen" because of the suffering on the cross, not in spite of it. Not for us to name it and claim it here, but to point us toward what will remain and what will last after this life. His promises are eternal, not just physical, and to preach anything else would need to be backed by still-living disciples and saints. In order to carry the weight of this world, we have to remember there is life after it.

As I spent time on my son's last birthday picking out flowers for a gravestone instead of planning a celebration of birth with cake and ice cream, my heart wanted to reenact the scene of Jesus flipping tables. I had stumbled on a message of a "well-meaning" church declaring a message that was built on the back of that word "favor." To those in the room who were walking in abundance and healing, it would have stirred up their faith and confirmed the goodness of God, but to the other half of the room walking in heartache, it would have isolated them from the heart of the Father. Those kinds of messages are great if you're doing great, and damaging if you're feeling damaged. How do we reconcile a God who heals if we have the belief...with the realities we still carry after we walk out of the service?

I've had my fair share of miracles, and they are amazing but finite. Today's miracles are still punctuated by our graves, so we cannot lose focus on the outcome that actually matters. Like never before has the purpose of the cross been so real and prevalent in my heart.

Jesus made sure life doesn't end here on earth, which is what I needed to know when my son died. I didn't need some patented phrase or loud declaration; I needed (still need) the shadow of the Most High. I need the shadow of the cross—the reminder that my darkness is surrounded by light. I need the promise and the protection of a long-suffering God who seeks me and finds me—even in spite of me. I need a God who writes in the sand in the face of my enemies (John 8:7), sits with me by the well (John 4), and has sweat drops of blood but still wipes my tears (Luke 22:44). Give me men and women who wash feet (and wash hair). Who out-love each other.

As a little girl, I was once picked to be the costume model for the Sunday School lesson on the Armor of God. Being a girl who grew up in an Independent Baptist church in the eighties, that's saying something. I proudly stood pointing out my helmet of salvation, my breastplate of righteousness, the belt of truth, shield of faith, and feet of peace. I felt strong and confident in my lightweight plastic props but didn't realize how heavy metal and iron would actually feel when forced to wear it and *use* it in a real battle.

In these next few chapters, I want us to look at some of the most "favored" people of the Bible, those spiritual giants that don the pages of the Bible stories we heard as kids. Unlike the victorious moments we seem to focus on and were shared by some of those great heroes in our Bible stories, I want us to dig a little deeper. I want us to see if maybe when God gives us the strength for the victory, He also gives us the strength for the pain. More than that, He helps us carry it, hold it, and heal from it so that we see others differently and Him differently. He is unlike any other God you've read about. He never asks us to carry anything He doesn't carry Himself.

Chapter 3

Did She Know?

As a young girl, I had a closeness with God. I can't quite explain it, but I can remember from a very young age crying out to God alone in my bedroom—not led by anyone else to do so but in the quietness of my own heart. Some of life's hurts and experiences I had seen and faced from a very young age drew me close to Him. I vividly remember at just five years old asking Jesus into my life. Looking back, it may have been the flannel-board graphics in Sunday School of hell's flames at the bottom and the white fluffy cotton-ball heaven and angel at the top that truly grabbed my attention and made my decision a no-brainer. I didn't need to be a rocket scientist to pick Door #1. Honestly though, beyond that, I had a closeness I can't quite explain, and I felt special to God. I felt like His girl.

I can remember reading about the story of Mary in my own little pink Bible and seeing those words, "highly favored." Mary is first mentioned in Matthew 1:18 and Luke 1:26, and her story pervades much of the Gospels and the book of Acts. At just seven or eight years old, my idea of "highly favored" was like being the teacher's chosen, the popular person, the *better-than-others* person. At that age, I had no concept of social ostracization, implication of infidelity, or the burden of carrying the *Holy Spirit's* baby Savior.

The angel went to her and said, "Greetings, you who are highly favored! The Lord is with you." Mary was greatly troubled at his words and wondered what kind of greeting this might be. But the angel said to her, "Do not be afraid, Mary; you have found favor with God. You will conceive and give birth to a son, and you are to call him Jesus. He will be great and will be called the Son of the Most High. The Lord God will give him the throne of his father David, and he will reign over Jacob's descendants forever; his kingdom will never end." (Luke 1:28-33)

With no list of items to tick off or religious quotas to meet in that little bedroom with the canopy bed and *Strawberry Shortcake* sheets, I pondered. *I wonder if I would be picked like Mary? Was I that special?*

In the past few months, that favor I felt as a little girl has been swept away in a whirlpool of tears, yet God keeps bringing me back to her, back to Mary, back to her story and back to her "favor." Was her favor fair? Some look at her story and think like I did that she was special, better than others, and somehow "prepared" for the position. But Mary was just a teenage girl whom God chose to task with the single-most important pregnancy of the world. There were no benchmarks or standards she could possibly meet in order to earn such a position. She couldn't have studied for this role or read *What to Expect When You're Expecting a Savior.* Her faith is not particularly mentioned prior to this sudden change in trajectory. She was not, from what we know, extraordinary, but God used her in an extraordinary way.

Even crazier is that the role I viewed as special and better-than-others was absolutely exhausting and confusing and arduous. Her motherhood carried so many burdens we can never imagine or fully comprehend.

I'm sure you have heard the song "Mary Did You Know?" She was not told how the future of being the earthly mother of God would affect her years beyond His birth. (Although yes, the angel *did* tell her who she was carrying.)

What has baffled me (and what I am now curious about) is did she know that the title of "highly favored" would actually come with loss? That favor to carry greatness can also mean favor to carry grief?

While diving deeper into the story of Mary, it really struck me that as an evangelical, Baptist-turned-Pentecostal Christian girl (again, maybe a book for another day), I have been taught, in length, about so many characters of the Bible, and yet Mary is characteristically only spoken of near or around Christmas. She isn't a main character in most evangelical church teachings but mainly a background character to the manger, the angels, to the North Star (and let's not forget Santa). I have heard more about the wise men and their gifts that prophesy the cross than about the woman who carried the literal weight of the Savior of the world. I don't know if it's because the churches I grew up in wanted to be careful with Mary lest we begin to idolize her in any way, but looking deeper into what she endured as the mother of the one we say we strive to be, I believe her story deserves a deep dive. It deserves a true look at a mother's heart.

Mary was a young teenage girl betrothed to be married. Unexpectedly, she becomes pregnant, and Joseph doesn't know what to think. I'm sure he's hurt and wondering "How in the world do I save face in this small town?" as it says in Matthew 1:19: *being a just man and unwilling to put her to shame, he resolved to divorce her quietly.*

I've only lived in a small town for one year of my life, but you could call your neighborhood Facebook page or your HOA "Nazareth" and you'll get the idea. Maybe it's just mine, but in our area, nothing goes unnoticed from the neighborhood Facebook page, and in a small town, nothing goes unnoticed either. I imagine people tilted their heads at the news that sweet Mary was now with child. That God called her "highly favored," no less. I have to think Joseph, the "just" man in this scenario, got the side-eye more times than he could count for staying with her. Mary had to rely on the Lord to send an angel to the love of her life to convince him she hadn't been unfaithful.

The matter was out of her hands. She had no authority over what other people thought about her or what the small-town gossip or bathroom wall had written on it. She had no proof. There was no Holy Spirit DNA test or Jerry Springer to announce, "the Holy Spirit is the father!" *No, she was totally at the mercy of the one that had chosen her. She wasn't asked permission to be chosen, but she was chosen just the same.*

Mary then left that small town to stay with her cousin Elizabeth. She *flees* as it says in Luke 1:39-40:

> *"In those days Mary arose and went with haste into the hill country, to a town in Judah, and she entered the house of Zechariah and greeted Elizabeth."*

"In those days" and "with haste." It appears she wastes no time to get out of dodge and get to someplace she can nurture this new promise in isolation from others' perspectives. There may be more to this than first meets the eye. There may be valuable wisdom in what appears like running.

When God speaks to us about a promise and a purpose and others around us balk at it or question our purity or our motives, it may do us a world of good to surround ourselves with those who can strengthen us and remind us of who we are and what we are capable of carrying.

I was considered very young to be married at just nineteen, and practically a teen mom when I had a child at twenty-one! Yet because I was married, people didn't look at me the way they looked at Mary. I felt as though I was so grown up, and people treated me like I was grown up because I was married, yet looking back, I was just a baby. I truly wonder how I figured out how to be a mom when I hadn't quite figured out how to take care of myself.

About five months into my pregnancy, I got sick with some type of flu and couldn't keep anything down for days. I lost a lot of weight and was actually under the weight I had started my pregnancy. My fever skyrocketed, and the doctor decided due to dehydration and a very high temperature, I had to be hospitalized to monitor my baby boy's health as well as my own. Not able to get the fever to break, the doctor decided an in-depth sonogram and other tests were needed to make sure nothing was significantly wrong with the baby.

The results weren't great. After seeing some dark spots on the sonogram, they weren't sure if there had been any brain damage, and they also found something in the blood work that hinted at him possibly having another disorder. The doctor suggested I see a genetics counselor to decide if I wanted to terminate the pregnancy. I declined because I truly decided to lay it in God's hands and knew that no matter what, we were going to choose to love this baby God had blessed us with, even if it looked different than we thought or if time was limited with him.

But I would be lying if I didn't say I was still scared to death. Fear gripped me, and I was so concerned about my sweet little one and also what the future would hold. Thankfully, the doctors were wrong (or God performed a miracle), but either way, we were blessed to bring home a beautiful and healthy baby boy. That was my first realization that I had little—if any—control over these precious lives I was given the opportunity to love and steward.

Fear doesn't pick favorites; it comes to us all. I believe He reminds us so many times in His Word to not fear because He knows how many times we will end up having to face it. Fear is our response to what's dangerous, but how we perceive danger varies. Sure, lions and tigers and bears are frightening! (Oh my!) But so is the *idea*, the *reality*, that we do not have control.

God knows that. "Fear not" and "trust me" could be interchangeable phrases in most Bible verses. My study of His faithful favored ones continually requires me to stare my lack of trust with God's plans directly in the face. He doesn't dismiss that struggle or look down on us for bringing our wavering hearts or angry thoughts to Him. If anything, He welcomes it. He is capable of holding both our questions and His love for us at the very same time.

After riding a donkey for miles (if you have ever been pregnant, you can literally feel the pain in parts of your body at the very thought), and after the miraculous birth of Jesus, in the "highly favored" manger scene surrounded by hay and cattle, Mary and Joseph do as any good Jewish parents would do: They have Jesus circumcised and blessed. They take him to the temple to meet Simeon, who has been waiting with literal bated breath to bless this coming Messiah. One would think the trumpets would be blowing and the red carpet would be rolled out for this coming King, but it appears much more subdued and quiet than even a family christening or baby dedication. At first, the words coming from this prophet or priest seem to be everything favored Mary could hope for:

"Sovereign Lord, as you have promised,

you may now dismiss your servant in peace.
For my eyes have seen your salvation,
which you have prepared in the sight of all nations:
a light for revelation to the Gentiles,
and the glory of your people Israel."
(Luke 2:29-32)

In fact, it says right after those words were spoken, Mary and Joseph marveled at what was said about Him, their new son Jesus. Can you imagine their faces? Bright with smiles and puffed-up chests about this light and glory that they get to care for? Their son. We can get cheesy and puffed up when our kid kicks a soccer goal or gets an A+ on a paper, but this child was going to be the salvation for the nations.

The funny thing is fear doesn't exist unless we know something is beyond our control.

When I was in that hospital bed, I was fine knowing I was caring for a little boy in my womb. I was fine being sick and not worried at all about my own health. It wasn't until the possibility of him not being okay entered the picture that fear gripped me. It was beyond my control. His future was not then, never has been, and nor ever will be in my hands.

Simeon, after speaking words of blessing, quickly turns his conversation from praising God to addressing Mary:

"This child is destined to cause the falling and rising of many in Israel, and to be <u>a sign that will be spoken against</u>, so that the thoughts of many hearts will be revealed. <u>And a sword will pierce your own soul too.</u>"

(Luke 2:34-35, emphasis added)

A sword will pierce your own soul too. *Too?* Well, throw a christening party and cut the cake! Does that sound like a blessing or a curse? Can you imagine what those words must have meant to His mother?

Mary's death is not recorded in Scripture. We don't know whether or not this term was used literally or figuratively because of the pain she would later experience in her own soul, but these words seem like a prophecy to what would happen to her precious baby.

I pause here to pray for the mamas carrying the heavy and yet holy weight (even though I'm sure it feels unholy) of caring for a child with a terminal prognosis or illness. You may well know what she felt in that moment. The questions of when, and how and why must have flooded her mind, and yet she was favored to carry it. *God knew the girl He had chosen would not crumble under the weight of the fear or the desire to understand but would be faithful to not only carry it, but carry it well.*

Carrying something well does not mean there are no emotions attached throughout the process. Sometimes what's out of our control can still make us feel guilty, as though we should have the superhuman ability to predict and prevent tragedy.

In the aftermath of the accident, everyone held grief differently, but we were all holding it. We were all holding a burning-hot, itchy, needle-point ball of hurt. I feel immense guilt and shame that someone else is in this place too. That because my son and his girlfriend were together when the accident happened, we all have to experience this loss.

I would do anything to have taken their place. Even though it was completely beyond my control, it feels too heavy to carry and the shame that comes with that is crushing. Sleepless nights, social anxiety, and fears have done nothing to help but only multiply my own grief and trauma, and yet it remains.

As we fast-forward a couple years into the story of Mary "the favored," I can only imagine she must have felt much the same. After all, Matthew shares that King Herod was after her child (the Savior), and to increase his chances of removing the threat to his throne, ordered *all* children under the age of two be killed.

> *"When Herod realized that he had been outwitted by the Magi, he was furious, and he gave orders to kill all the boys in Bethlehem and its vicinity who were two years old and under, in accordance with the time he had learned from the Magi."*

(Matthew 2:16)

Mary was startled awake by a dream her husband had by another angel, who said they must flee. I'm assuming she was only able to grab the essentials that would fit her and her now-toddler son onto a donkey with no trunk space as they fled to Egypt.

Phew! Great! Grand! They are safe and the favor of the Lord came to them in a dream. Where's the shame in that?

Herod had cast a wide net, and many innocent lives were lost as a result.

> *Then what was said through the prophet Jeremiah was fulfilled:*
> *"A voice is heard in Ramah,*
> *weeping and great mourning,*
> *Rachel weeping for her children*
> *and refusing to be comforted,*
> *because they are no more."* (v. 18)

Theologians much smarter than myself estimate that about two to three thousand people were in Bethlehem and all the surrounding area. That's not many people. The very people Mary would have loved, hung out with, had playdates with (if they did that sort of thing), went to the well with, and swapped recipes with would have been the very ones targeted by Herod because of her son.

Can you imagine as they fled through the night what horrible thoughts she would have had to endure as she pictured the little ones of her friends she so loved? The weight she had to carry as she ran in the middle of the night, knowing other children the same age as her young would be brutal targets of an insecure king? It makes my chest hurt as a grieving mama at all the loss but also the weight our dear Mary had to carry. A weight that was not her fault and yet hers all the same. A weight that, given the option, she would certainly have turned into a different outcome.

But just as fear does not discriminate or pick favorites, neither does shame and guilt. What-ifs and whys can cripple our here-and-nows if we remain in them. The things we cannot change will leave us absolutely frozen in fear and sadness if we don't continue to take another step and choose the next right thing. Trust me I understand that battle all too well.

Mary was "favored" with purpose to carry the Savior, "favored" with protection, but "favored" also with the burden of danger, of grief, and of shame. The only way to carry that much weight is with eyes locked on the heavenly Father.

What I am realizing is just because I don't like something this world throws at me doesn't mean I have any authority over it or any ability to change it, and the only thing I can do is be honest through it. Truly. I can pray just as Jesus Himself said to His father, *"My Father, if it be possible, let this cup pass from me"* (Matthew 26:39). But it is so much harder for me to utter the last of the words He spoke to His Father. *"Nevertheless, not as I will, but as you will."*

nev·er·the·less

adverb

in <u>spite</u> of that; <u>notwithstanding</u>; all the same.

In spite of my desire and my wishes, not as I will but as you will. There are so many things I wish we didn't have to face in this world. Loss and death exceedingly and abundantly outweighs them all. It doesn't elude my thoughts that the two choices we are truly given this side of heaven are to either suffer or suffer well.

"Suffer well." Even those words make the bile rise in my throat because is there truly such a thing? As we look at the heart of Mary, the woman, the mother, I believe we see that she truly wasn't a robotic, angelic being that had no real human emotion or grief. No. We see a real woman looking into the eyes of her son, the son she raised and the son she loved, and we see a mother who would do as any mother would do. I believe if she could have, she would have done anything to take His place.

> *Near the cross of Jesus stood his mother, his mother's sister, Mary the wife of Clopas, and Mary Magdalene. When Jesus saw his mother there, and the disciple whom he loved standing nearby, he said to her, "Woman, here is your son," and to the disciple, "Here is your mother." From that time on, this disciple took her into his home.*

(John 19:25-27)

One thing that I have never heard any family member, friend, or pastor want to do is be present at someone's death bed. Do they do it? Absolutely. But from my experience, it has only been for two reasons: out of necessity (because it's your job) or out of love. No one with a sane mind is attracted to suffering or grief.

In the verses above, we see Mary, her sister, and three others. They are not there because they want to be. They are there because there is nowhere else to be. The one they love is there, and they won't leave Him. Love gives you the capacity to bear the unthinkable. This is the picture of a mother's heart. I fully believe she would have done anything to take Him off that cross, just as I would do anything to change this chapter of my life, *but if I'm learning anything it is that if the grave even came to the Savior of the world, we don't get an exemption.*

In studying Mary, I would be lying if I said it doesn't bother me that the scriptures don't give us a picture of Jesus revealing Himself to His mother after His death. If I had scripted it out (and you can be thankful I wasn't asked), I would have had her there before anyone else, weeping with joy at the sight of her son alive, but the scriptures don't give us that. I can't be sure why they don't, but what I can be sure of is that she already believed what He had said and was truly given the opportunity of having a front-row seat at raising the Son of God. She was the very woman who spoke up at the wedding and said:

> *"They have no wine." And Jesus said to her, "Woman, what does this have to do with me? My hour has not yet come." His mother said to the servants, "Do whatever he tells you."*
>
> *Now there were six stone water jars there for the Jewish rites of purification,*

each holding twenty or thirty gallons. Jesus said to the servants, "Fill the jars with water." And they filled them up to the brim. And he said to them, "Now draw some out and take it to the master of the feast."

(John 2:3-8, emphasis added)

Now, we could just breeze past this fact that this first miracle was prompted by His mother's words, but have you ever had a son look at you and start his sentence with "woman"? I can't recall any of my three boys being brave enough to do so, but I wish we could have had a close-up shot of her face at that exact moment. Many scholars postulate that "woman" in Hebrew is actually a term of endearment, but my gut reaction was still shock! I guess the sinless Lamb of God wasn't about to be disobedient to His mother because the very next thing we see is Mary telling the servants: "Do whatever He tells you."

She knew who He was. She had no doubt. She had seen His gifts and humble spirit. She had believed what God had said about her son and knew who He truly was. Did it make what she had to carry any easier? I don't believe so but she had positioned her heart to not only suffer, but to suffer well. She called out the things in her son God had told her about Him. She was a good mother that spoke up and stood firm on the destiny placed on her lap. Oh how thankful I am for the blessings He placed on mine. Although my dramatic cinematic version of what happened after the cross would appear better in my own heart and eyes, there was no reason for Jesus to prove to Mary what was to come or that He was resurrected. She knew the story, and she fully believed it.

She was favored enough to carry the grief that accompanied the cross because she knew what it meant. It not only meant that He would be raised again. It also meant that for a mother many, many years later, typing words on a tear-stained desk, just doing my own best to suffer well, there was more. It would mean the difference between heaven and hell. It would mean that she would have to wait a lifetime to see her son again, but that I would also be allowed to see my son again. It would mean eternity. She truly carried the weight of the words with full belief that *this life is all for everything or nothing at all.*

If I am learning anything in this life, it is as Ecclesiastes states, *"but a vapor"* (1:2). Life is "but a vapor," as Solomon writes. This life isn't the end. The goodness of God doesn't end when we lose one of our greatest blessings here on earth. What we do in this life truly means everything or it means nothing at all, and I have declared in my own heart it means everything. That is the hope of the cross. I want to share that hope with so many others that heaven looks different, looks *crowded.* In Hebrews 12:1-2, the writer mentions a "cloud of witnesses" that welcome those who enter heaven:

> *Therefore, since we are surrounded by so great a cloud of witnesses, let us also lay aside every weight and the sin that clings so closely, and let us run with perseverance the race that is set before us, looking to Jesus, the pioneer and perfecter of faith, who for the sake of the joy that was set before him endured the cross, disregarding its shame, and has taken his seat at the right hand of the throne of God.*

I take this as a reason to press into God in my grief. When I choose loyalty to God and His promises, I'm not invalidating or refusing my pain. I'm choosing to carry it with company, with the hope that it will change how others get to see God, experience God, and choose Him too. Will we make heaven look different because of our loss or be lost in suffering?

Chapter 4

Just Call Me Bitter

I've had many nicknames in life. Some I've liked, some I didn't mind, and others I truly despised. As a young girl, I was quite round, and by "quite," I mean *very*. It took a few years to grow into my chubby little body, but eventually my height matched my rolls and extra fluff with the exception of one spot on my little frame—my cheeks. They say one of the easiest ways to humble yourself is to have children, and my boys, true to form, spared no expense of my feelings as they looked back at my childhood department store pics.

"Mom, why is your head shaped like a peanut?"

"Mom, your cheeks look like you were storing away for winter."

What can I say? They weren't wrong. My dad had given me the cute pet name of "fat stuff" as a little one, and about the time I started rounding (pun intended) the corner toward my middle school years, my mom was wise enough to point out, "Maybe we should change that nickname. It's not so cute anymore." (Thank you, Mom). The name, of course, was just a cute pet name that I actually look back on and smile with fondness, but many times in life, we are given names that carry weight. We are given names that stick. I've been the jock, the cheerleader, the pastor's wife, the mean girl, the nice girl, so-and-so's mom, and many more. At this point in my life, I have come to realize the titles, nicknames, and things people have called me aren't necessarily the ones that carry the most weight. The names I have the hardest time shaking are the ones I give myself.

Whether it be a name someone else has called me, the name I have adopted, or the name made up out of my own volition, names matter. They define us. They give us an identity. My first name, for example, is a pretty different name, and in all my years, I've only met a handful of other people with the same name, and even then, not one of them has had the same spelling. It isn't found in any baby name book, nor does it have any predetermined meaning attached to it. It's a name smushed together from two other names (Janette and Dena—old friends of my mom). Having a "different" name growing up in the eighties meant that I wouldn't find it on the keychain or bicycle license plate in any gift shop on a school field trip. It also meant it would be mispronounced and commonly misspelled. I had a softball trophy, for example, that was awarded to "Keanette." Come on, coach. That wasn't even close. And let's not even mention I played ball for you for years? But I digress. Names matter.

When we run into someone we haven't seen for a while, what is the first thing we try so hard to do? Remember their name. We know the importance and how we feel when someone remembers our name, and we also know what it feels like when they don't. I want to take a closer look at a woman that had a fine name but decided to change it to something else.

Naomi.

Over the years, I have read the book of Ruth numerous times and have always been enamored with the story of God's provision and the kinsman redeemer Boaz (who I think we all picture as some gorgeous knight in shining armor riding horseback during sunset through the wheat field saying "glean here, pretty lady" or maybe that's just me, and this definitely isn't that kind of book). In all my years of hearing the story, I have grazed right past the depth of Naomi. Who has time for that part of the story? Who wants to dig into all that she had to lose in order for the beautiful silver lining at the end? Who wants to watch a fairytale without a happy ending?

If we aren't careful we can easily put the struggles of the real people, important enough to have their name and history jotted down on those parchment papers, relegated to the sad arch of some fairytale. We can see the purpose of the pain as part of a bigger plot to get to the promise and not as the main story itself. As I dug deeper into her story, I ran across something I had never noticed before but that so resonated in my soul:

> *"Don't call me Naomi," she told them. "Call me Mara, because the Almighty has made my life very bitter. I went away full, but the LORD has brought me back empty. Why call me Naomi? The LORD has afflicted me; the Almighty has brought misfortune upon me."*

(Ruth 1:20-21)

As she utters these words, I can only imagine her saying it with anger and a guttural cry. "My name is no longer Naomi, my name is Mara (bitter)." She is in mourning. She is trying to find her new identity. I wish I could say I couldn't relate to her feelings, but I see so much of her in me.

As a family, we have taken many leaps of faith. Some that felt like they were lined up for miles before we took the first step (those are easy), and some that felt like we were stepping off a cliff, covered in fog, while blind folded, not knowing if there was anything there to catch us. What I have come to realize is no matter how big the step of faith He asks us to take, it always feels uncomfortable, and there will almost always be loss attached. Whether it's loss of friendships, titles, expectations, or great grand heartbreaking loss, the biggest steps are built on a foundation of hard things.

In the first chapter of Ruth, we see Naomi, her husband, and their two sons leave Bethlehem to Moab to try to outrun a famine. Her husband then dies, and she is left with her two sons who decide to stay and who then take Moabite wives. They left their comforts of Bethlehem under their father's leadership, but they stayed there under hers.

Everything had seemed just fine and dandy. Her grief regarding the loss of her husband isn't really recorded, and life just seems to keep moving for her and her sons for about ten years until she loses not one but both of them as well. She's lost them all. She has lost everything she came with. She left the comforts of Bethlehem with her husband seeking safety only to have the very place she sought out be the grave of everyone she loved. In her own words, *"she went away (from Bethlehem) full and came back empty."*

A famous stage of grief is called "bargaining," in which the sufferer wonders what little detail could have changed all the tragedy. Naomi's tone in these first two chapters of Ruth give me everything I need to know. She was struggling with bargaining as well. What if her husband hadn't made that choice? What if they had stayed in Bethlehem? What if she had chosen to return sooner? She looks now at both of her daughters-in-law, the only two she has in her life and tells them:

"Go back, each of you, to your mother's home. May the LORD show you

kindness, as you have shown kindness to your dead husbands and to me. May the LORD grant that each of you will find rest in the home of another husband."

Then she kissed them goodbye and they wept aloud and said to her, "We will go back with you to your people."

But Naomi said, "Return home, my daughters. Why would you come with me? Am I going to have any more sons, who could become your husbands? Return home, my daughters; I am too old to have another husband. Even if I thought there was still hope for me—even if I had a husband tonight and then gave birth to sons— would you wait until they grew up? Would you remain unmarried for them? No, my daughters. <u>It is more bitter for me than for you, because the LORD's hand has turned against me!</u>"

(Ruth 1:8-13, emphasis added)

She has nothing left to offer. She has nothing left to give. She is not only mourning but has no one to fight for her besides herself and the God she isn't sure she can trust. She doesn't stand on some platform and declare the goodness of God in this moment; she tells these two women looking to her for guidance that the hand of the Lord is against her and to go back home. She feels like God has turned His back on her and even wonders if she is to blame. She doesn't even want to see how hard this is for them; she is lost in her own grief and can't see anything but her own despair. *"It is more bitter for me than for you."* She feels as if the God she has introduced them to has let her down and turned His back on them all.

Just call me bitter.

Many times in the Bible, we see people change their name, and most often it is given from the Lord, but that's what makes this name change so significant to me. It's a name she gave herself. God never once in the Word says her loss was a punishment, that she did anything wrong, or that He took their lives because they should have never been in Moab. Theologians can debate all day long the reasons they should have or shouldn't have moved to the land, but the Bible never states that the Lord was angry, withdrew His hand, or "turned against them," yet here she is declaring it as truth.

In her eyes, her circumstances enforce the belief that the Lord hasn't shown her kindness, so she fears she may be the negative in the equation. She knows God has the power to give and to take away, and in this moment, He chose the latter. She is hell-bent on trying to understand it. *When we walk through things we don't understand, the easiest thing to do is be angry and blame the one in control of it all.*

Naomi crying out, "go back to your own mothers" carries more weight than just telling these girls she didn't have provision for them. She was telling them to go back to the way they were before they had met her and before they had met her sons. She was telling them to go back to the god of the Moabites, Chemosh (Kamōš), who was a Baal-like god known for child/human sacrifice. Was she simply trying to look out for their best interest when it came to this famine? Or was she debating whether or not they were just as well off to return to another god? *Grief and loss have a way of making you look directly in the face of what you believe, not wavering, not looking away but head on to see if it will hold up under the pressure of your new surroundings, your new name, and your new identity.* She was now the bitter, childless widow.

Orpah kisses her mother-in-law and returns home. Naomi makes one more hard push for Ruth to do the same:

"Look," said Naomi, "your sister-in-law is going back to her people and her gods. Go back with her."

But Ruth replied, "Don't urge me to leave you or to turn back from you. Where you go I will go, and where you stay I will stay. Your people will be my people and your God my God. Where you die I will die, and there I will be buried. May the LORD deal with me, be it ever so severely, if even death separates you and me." When Naomi realized that Ruth was determined to go with her, she stopped urging her.

(Ruth 1:15-18)

Naomi did her best to deter Ruth, but it appears Ruth realized that to go with her mother-in-law with nothing was better than to return to her family's god with the possibility of plenty. Even in her own grief and loss, she was standing firm on the promises of her new family and her new bloodline. *"If even death separates you and me…"* This was a faith declaration. She was clinging to what she could see in Naomi and her God, even when her mother-in-law couldn't see it for herself.

God doesn't pick favorites and is no respecter of persons. Ruth the Moabite stands in the looming gap holding tightly to Naomi reminding her of what faithfulness looks like. Faithfulness is not always proved by provision and abundance. Faithfulness is found in knowing who you really are and walking it out regardless of your circumstances. If we build a faith only on what our God will give us and only follow Him as He answers our prayers to meet our demands, we have done nothing more than relegate His strength, knowledge, and power to a puny genie in a bottle, waiting for us to require something of Him. Making ourselves the god.

And so the childless widow and her daughter-in-law return to

Bethlehem with nothing to their name and on the very bottom of the cultural ladder. Hundreds of years later, another unmarried young mother would come up pregnant carrying the Savior in the very same town. These two come striding in causing quite a stir. The whole town (remember how small towns talk) is a-buzz saying, "Is this Naomi?" She corrects them and gives her new name, her new self-given name: "Call me Mara."

No one is ever documented actually calling her this new name besides herself. In fact, she says, "Call me Mara," and the very next verse says: "so Naomi returned." I believe we get all attributes from God, so even our sense of humor is from Him. It makes me chuckle. I can see it now, her declaring "Call me Mara!" with a guttural cry, and the one jotting down the text rolls His eyes and starts the next sentence, "so *Naomi* returned…"

Now lest we look at Naomi and shake our heads at her giving herself this new name, I find great comfort in this. We see no proof that she is chastised or looked down upon because of what she believes about her new life. God doesn't correct her or punish her. He doesn't rush her through her grief or tell her to get her act together. He just simply calls her by her real name. *He is strong enough to hold onto us when we climb down into our valley and our self-prescribed pity parties, but He is also holy enough to remind us of who we really are.*

Oftentimes when we are at our lowest points in life, looking at those around us on their mountaintops (or at the very least, Insta-filtered peaks plastered on social media pages), it can feel daunting to do anything. We can feel stuck, frozen, and unable to take any step at all because anything we accomplish would feel like a splash in the bucket (a very large bucket the size of an ocean). Naomi seems to be stuck. Ruth comes to her and asks permission to do the only thing she can think of to help them not starve; she asks to go glean in one of the fields of a distant relative of Naomi's.

We live in a town near Plant City, Florida. With a population of just under forty thousand people, they are known for one thing and pretty much one thing only: strawberries. Plant City (aptly named) is nicknamed the strawberry capital of the world. It comes complete with a country fair, amazing country bands from all over the sweet south, and of course, the Strawberry Queen. This is a local favorite, and many people enjoy it much more than the Florida State Fair not far away. It's much smaller, feels more family friendly, and comes complete with the world's best strawberry shortcake (at least so they claim).

Every year for many years, when my boys were younger, we would ride the rides and eat the corn dogs, and even stand in line for the world's best strawberry shortcake, but we would never buy the strawberries from there. Why? Because it was much cheaper to go to the U-Pick down the road and pick the stragglers yourself. Easier? No. Cooler? Absolutely not. But cheaper? Bingo. It was also a beautiful memory and an experience. I would usually give the farmer a little extra cash at the end of my family running amuck through his field because honestly, I had no idea how many berries made it into my boy's mouth instead of their little buckets. I would purposefully seek out the organic growers because I knew my boys would strut right past my warning of pesticides and dirt and pop them in their mouths regardless. The red juice running down their chins was always a telltale sign they had pre-tasted their loot. The memories were worth it but some years, it was a lot of work. Those fields had been well-reaped by the professionals. We had to hunt high and low to find berries that weren't rotting and still good enough to eat.

The professional reapers were very good at what they were assigned to do and left very little behind.

It's in a similar field, a well-gleaned field, that we find Ruth. She was gleaning after professional reapers, looking for any scraps that may have been left behind, but one thing was missing: the U-pick sign. Without paying a price ahead of time or doing an internet search for whether the farmer was a fan of the public coming onto his private property, Ruth goes out in hopes that there is something she can find to help them put food in their empty bellies.

This could have posed real trouble for her, and at the very least, she could have been harshly run off the land. Naomi, the actual relative and past citizen of Bethlehem, doesn't join her, and we don't know why. Was she too weak or too old for working in the field? Did she think the risk wouldn't be worth the reward? Maybe. But couldn't she have at least gone to her relative on Ruth's behalf and asked his permission? Let's not forget her daughter-in-law was a foreigner. Naomi would have known the land, the people, and also the risks.

As a teenage girl, I wasn't scared of much. Honestly, looking back, there were many times I walked right through a warning that I should have yielded to. I feel sorry in a way for my kids and the generations that come behind because I'm not sure there will ever be another group of teens or kids again that won't have everything they do documented on social media and every move they make traced. We were the wild ones. The ones that played until the street lights came on or out in the woods, making up fairytales and looking for treasures with nothing more connecting us to home than a time to be back for dinner.

It was on one of those "treasure-seeking" hot summer days in the woods of North Carolina my dear friend Jill and I found ourselves doing exactly what my dad had warned us not to do. We were thrill-seeking teenage girls who hadn't quite earned our driver's licenses but found freedom blowing in our hair on the back of a muddy four-wheeler. We had done the usual paths and seen the usual things and decided against my dad's best advice to stay on the beaten trail when we saw a bumpy, unkempt dirt road.

With a smile and a nod at each other (okay maybe more from me than Jill), we turned onto it to see where it led. We were laughing hysterically as we almost got stuck numerous times on what seemed to be a road meant more to keep people out than to welcome them home. This should have been a good sign, but with brains not fully developed and more adventure in our bones than sense, we kept driving. Those laughs quickly stopped as a man popped out of the woods dressed like a character from the Beverly Hillbillies (before they moved to Beverly) complete with a long-nosed shotgun.

As I struggled to get that four-wheeler into reverse, my passenger went full Pentecostal mode and started speaking in tongues at the top of her lungs as he let us know, "Y'all ain't welcome in these parts!" As we tore out of there and ran back into the house with the screen door slamming behind us, confessing every single one of our wild child ways and disobedient sins that day, I can still hear my dad just belly-laughing at us. He was thankful we were safe, but he knew we had learned a greater lesson than any lesson he could have ever taught us. Dad knew the land. He knew there were moonshine factories up those mountains that were (as we can attest to) protected. He knew the risks because he was familiar with the area and had made sure we knew them as well.

I believe just the same that Naomi would have been the better candidate to glean. She could have at least attended to her daughter-in-law and let her know where it was safe and where it wasn't, but she is nowhere to be found and sends her out with little more than "go ahead my daughter." Why?

I tend to believe Naomi was stuck. Stuck in grief, not truly caring if they lived or if they died. Grief and loss have a way of doing that to one's soul. She didn't have the motivation or the energy to take the next right step, but her daughter-in-law took a step for them both. There may be seasons in which we carry others and there may be seasons others carry us. This is why it's important for us to allow other people into our corner. It's also the reason we should be picky about who we allow to join us when we are backed into a corner.

In comes the knight and shining armor, Boaz. He sees Ruth gleaning, and tells his men and women to leave more behind for her as he takes notice of all she has done for Naomi. He makes sure she is well-fed and protected, then tells her to glean from his fields only. As Ruth gets home with what is evidently more than she should have picked from a barren field, Naomi takes notice and asks, *"Where did you glean today? And where have you worked? Blessed be the man who took notice of you?"* (2:19).

In this moment, we see Naomi slightly nudge from bitterness to blessing. All of a sudden, there is a shift in her. Her stomach now full, she blesses the man who found favor on her daughter-in-law. Don't let this moment slip pass without seeing the gravity of it. Who is she blessing? Boaz. Yes, but more importantly, who is she blessing him with? God. *A blessing is only as powerful as the name, purpose, and belief behind it. She is still working out her own pain, loss, and grief, but deep down inside, when faced with a glimpse of hope, she does not hold back who she finds her hope in.* From bitter to blessed with one ephah of barley, even in our darkest moments, what we truly believe will come out in our actions. *"For out of the abundance of the heart the mouth speaks"* (Luke 6:45). (A good comforting meal doesn't hurt either.)

We begin to see the narrative shift after this moment. Many theologians take up an opinion on Naomi's advice to Ruth. Some believe she may have been overbearing and pushed the narrative with her suggestions to her daughter-in-law and yet some applaud her. Her counsel for Ruth to go sneak into Boaz on the men's threshing room floor could have been seen as scandalous and was definitely not the cultural norm. After the encounter, we see him tell those in the room *"Let it not be known that the woman came to the threshing floor."*

Could God have miraculously provided the kinsman redeemer without Naomi's interference? Of course He could have, yet He chooses to use her newfound hope and strength and blesses her actions immensely. Throughout the entirety of the book of Ruth, we see Naomi's struggle with the Lord. It's a beautiful, raw picture of the faith we have to fight so hard to keep while walking through the realities of this life here on earth. She was finding her fight. She was pushing through the bitterness, seeking not a man for her daughter-in-law but rest, peace, and security (3:1).

I wonder if the theologians reading this same script—but about a *man* taking those same scary steps of faith or pushing their son or son-in-law into a place of possible danger—would have deemed it as brave and heroic instead of pushy or overbearing?

This woman was not only strong enough to make it out of her trials and losses in life but fight through her trust issues with the God she served. She is working out her own faith. She is hashing it out with God, and we see her life go from great calamity to greater capacity.

When you have lost everything, there is nothing holding you back. When you have nothing left to lose, you won't fear what happens next. You find strength in knowing nothing can hurt you greater than you have already been hurt, and you find the power to fight hell and the narrative of the names given to you by others or even given to you by yourself.

Naomi should have never been known. She had no husband and no son to carry on her name. The "Bitter Childless Widow" should have been on her gravestone (and the title of her scripture passage), but she becomes the owner of the property from Boaz. No fruit should have come from her life because she had no seed, no child left living, but she is given value even in this ancient patriarchal society. She stumbled back into Bethlehem with no husband and no sons, but her beloved foreign daughter-in-law became the great-grandmother of King David and in the direct lineage of a Savior, our Savior. Heartache and suffering will impact generations. Whether or not they impact generations for good or for bad is up to us when faced with those decisions. Physical loss (however great it may be) will never be bigger than spiritual loss, and every choice made impacts eternity. Our value is found in Him alone and in how we choose to carry it.

I used to think of the story of Ruth and Boaz as the "happy ending"— the fairytale we all hoped to be true in our own stories. What I realize now is the promise Boaz brought with him didn't take away from what they had already lost. He didn't replace the heartache. He didn't replace Naomi's sons or Ruth's husband. He is a picture of the promise we all have, regardless of our story.

Regardless of whether or not we have some distant relative here on earth with land and resources who lets us come to their U-pick farm for free; we have a kinsman redeemer who has a different address and a different seat. He sits at the right hand of the Father and doesn't just own a little land; He owns it all. He doesn't just feel bad for our suffering and our loss. He sits in it with us and redeems it not by the sweat of His labor but with His own blood. He doesn't mind our unfiltered and possibly unflattering attempts to get to Him. He sees us fighting to find rest, peace, and security in His arms. He won't label us as pushy or overbearing when we fight to make our way to Him. He ignores the labels we give ourselves with arms stretched out—wiping our tears, ready to welcome us, redeem us, and remind us of who we really are: His.

> *"I have told you these things, so that in me you may have peace. In this world you will have trouble. But take heart! I have overcome the world."*

(John 16:33)

Highly Favored

Chapter 5

Twosies

Picture it with me. You are walking the halls of the church in the late eighties, maybe early nineties. Some sweet soul has been painstakingly donning the rough-textured stucco walls of the nursery corridor with murals of all the great stories of the Bible. Adam and Eve walk the Garden (with impeccable leaf placement, of course), David holds his slingshot, Daniel survives in the lion's den, and the *pièce de resistance*—Noah's Ark.

The colorful rainbow beautifully arched over the entrance of the vessel lights the way for the mommy and daddy animals to walk in—you guessed it—two by two. As a bi-product of growing up in kids church during that era, there is a song that will forever live rent-free in my brain (if you did too, you can thank me for now having it stuck in your head the rest of the day):

> *The animals, the animals*
>
> *They came in by twosies, twosies*
>
> *The animals, the animals*
>
> *They came in by twosies, twosies*
>
> *Elephants and kangaroosies, roosies*
>
> *Children of the Lord*

It's a cute song, complete with lyrics that end by stating everything turns out hunky dory. But in these murals, I noticed something. Kids were looking at rainbows and triumphs without much acknowledgement of the work it took to get there. Now, please hear me. This isn't me bashing anyone's church nursery decor or wanting us to deconstruct our children's wing murals. Certainly I am not suggesting we scar children with biblically accurate portrayals of murder and violence. I do wonder though if from a very young age, our eyes aren't drawn to the rainbow before realizing what was endured to get there. Working in children's ministry for years and years, I met so many little ones with heartbreak not even adults should have to experience, and (it felt like) my job was to promise it all works itself out because in the end, doves bring olive branches. Now it feels like I was part of bait-and-switch scheme. Did we set them up for confusion? In our desire to see the goodness of God and teach others about the goodness of God, we have begun to shy away from the hard parts of the story.

Children's ministry was one of my favorite places to serve in the church. There's just nothing like it. It is no wonder to me why Jesus loved the littles and wanted them to come close. I taught the same age at children's church for years: first grade. My "little firsties" as I called them would come in at the beginning of the year, timid, barely able to read but would finish the year strong and confident. Overflowing with wonder and *tons* of questions, you quickly realize there is no Jr. Holy Spirit (as Pastor Tracy would always say). They could ask some of the toughest questions and also want prayer for some of the deepest and realest prayer requests. In the first grader's world, there is no such thing as the well-touted "unspoken prayer request." That request you more often hear from teenagers or adults, and it typically means, "I want

someone to know something is wrong, but I want to seem mysterious."
No, in fact, the average first-grader is ready to spill all the tea. All. The.
Tea.

I got used to changing the subject or pulling aside the little tender
heart that thought the best place to share any family drama would be in
the confines of our little spot on the carpet while the other fifteen little
pairs of ears leaned in to try to hear every sordid detail. I also grew
grossly accustomed to the realization that teaching them only about
rainbows wouldn't help them have the strength to build arks. No, even
by first grade, I believe my little budding theologians would have given
me the side eye if I tried to tell them Grandma dying, Daddy leaving,
or their school being shut down again because of a pandemic or school
shooting threat was "all God's plan." These children that have been
instructed by teachers behind masks and been taught not just how to
tuck and roll by Smokey the Bear, but how to also hide from bullets
won't do well being taught the highlight reel of our Bible heroes. This
generation needs to be ark builders.

Children are intuitive little buggers, and I believe they can sniff a
platitude just as sharply as a grief-familiar adult. Instead of giving them
scripted responses to unimaginable hurt (and bypassing the humanity
and fragility of their experience), I started asking the Holy Spirit to tell
me what—in that moment, for that particular child—would be most
comforting, helpful, and compassionate. Maybe it is reassurance through
censored Bible stories, but a lot of times, it's actually acknowledging and
hugging and kicking our feet at the hard present reality.

The story of Noah is a hard reality. It's not easy to read that God
regretted creating the human race. Noah's obedience was not glamorous
or appreciated by others, but God noticed him. Being noticed by God

during an entire population's reckoning might seem like a nice pat on the back, but boy did it have strings attached.

> *The LORD saw how great the wickedness of the human race had become on the earth, and that every inclination of the thoughts of the human heart was only evil all the time. The LORD regretted that he had made human beings on the earth, and his heart was deeply troubled. So the LORD said, "I will wipe from the face of the earth the human race I have created—and with them the animals, the birds and the creatures that move along the ground—for I regret that I have made them."*
>
> *But Noah found <u>favor</u> in the eyes of the LORD.*

(Genesis 6:5-8, emphasis added)

The world was corrupt, and God regretted what humankind had become. Growing worse by the day, filled with corruption and violence (sound familiar?). In comes the hero, the "favored" Noah. Not dressed in armor but with tools in hand, ready to get to work. God decides this righteous man and his family will be the only ones He chooses to save.

Sometimes saving grace comes in the form of supernatural miracles, but more often than not, it comes with hard work. At well beyond retirement age, 500+ years old to be exact, we see God reveal the ticking clock to Noah, and He gives him a detailed map on how to save more than just his family but everyone else this side of history. Filled with long days and back-breaking work, Noah obediently and meticulously follows God's plan. He builds an ark.

Today it seems like no big deal when a new building is thrown up within days, weeks, or months. Just down the road from us, a huge new Amazon warehouse seemed to be birthed overnight, but this was not the case in Noah's day. With no drill in hand, no power tools, dump truck, or crane to rent, how was he able to build such a structure? The Bible isn't clear on how much he built on his own or how much he had help with the ark.

Being a family that also has three boys, I can with almost complete certainty assume his boys had their shoulders tapped more than once or twice to help with some of the heavy lifting. I can see the eye rolls from Shem, Ham, and Japheth and hear the sighing now: "Again dad? How much longer do we have to build this thing?" The boat took so long to build, Noah's sons were about to hit the centenarian marker themselves as the ark was completed. If this had been made into a true-to-life major motion picture, the trailer would have looked a lot less like the Russel Crowe version and a lot more like the 1985 trailer for *Cocoon*. Pretty par for the course for most of our Bible heroes and heroines, Noah and his family would not have been first picked in the line-up of any P.E. dodgeball game, and yet here they are saving humanity. God doesn't tout Noah's strength, engineering skills, or zoology degree as credence for his qualifications; He looks at the heart:

> *Noah was a righteous man, blameless among the people of his time, and he walked faithfully with God.*

(Genesis 6:9)

Our age, knowledge, and résumé will never dictate our destiny. They may help define our paycheck, but they will never define our purpose. As long as we have breath in our lungs and feet on this earth, He has more work for us to do here. Obedience is a lifelong assignment, but how quickly are we typically ready to throw in the towel when life takes us through hard things? Noah had lived a long life already. He had no guarantee his life would last for hundreds of more years. He knew what God had told Him up to that point and to that point only. He realized what was to become of him had less to do with him and more to do with those behind him. When we focus on those we love instead of ourselves, we become capable of carrying unimaginable weight. We grow strong enough to carry out callings that seem improbable and pass on eternal promises that seem impossible. We will impact more than just earthly generations and instead will help populate the heavens.

> *The animals going in were male and female of every living thing, as God had commanded Noah. Then the LORD shut him in.*

(Genesis 7:6)

Then the Lord shut him in.

I think we all remember where we were when we first heard about a pandemic and "two weeks to flatten the curve." I don't believe any of us really knew what to expect, and I can almost guarantee many had no idea what they would lose. Some dear to us lost loved ones, others lost businesses, and still others lost the ability to find peace of any sort because fear began to grow so viciously. You didn't have to venture far to see fear in someone's eyes. You just had to make a quick trip to the grocery store.

After facing our own searing tragic loss, I look back at that time being "shut in" with family as a peculiar blessing. We had what I deem as the most precious gift on earth and something that no matter how much you spend is never wasted—time together. We worked hard as a family trying to love on others during that season. Our entire family throughout those months were super involved in a local church that began to minister digitally. Daily, those in our household were busy making content after everyone was thrust online to stay connected. Filming videos for kids church, Marriage Mondays on Facebook Live to encourage marriages, daily devotionals, and live call-in prayer services became the new norm. We did our best to try to be a light during such a dark time. Different seasons have a way of developing new muscles you never knew you had, even if you didn't ask to work them out.

I can't imagine what it must have been like for Noah to have been shut in with no access to the outside world or with no capability to help those around him. They were totally isolated.

The Bible says he was blameless among the people of his time. Noah had to have been like a blaring light in the darkness to his community for God to have given him a title such as blameless; filled with love and compassion in a world God said was so tainted He needed to wipe it clean. I've heard it preached that Noah must have been ridiculed for building such a structure, but the Word doesn't actually say that. It just says he was blameless among the people. Innocent of any wrongdoing in a generation determined to fulfill every selfish pleasure, Noah remained faithful, and the people around him knew it. There is a vast difference between being righteous and self-righteous. Noah was labeled the first.

Why would the Lord have asked Noah to do so much work and then choose to shut the door for him? Was it too heavy? Was Noah not strong enough? Was there no way for the door to be opened? I believe God didn't want Noah to have to take the step of closing the door on the very people he would have been serving; the people that saw him as blameless. God was gracious enough to do that for him, but also empowering enough to allow Noah to open the door back up to freedom on the other side of such devastating loss (Genesis 8).

This picture, although gruesome to think about, is a great reminder that vengeance is not ours to take. Our job is to love and love well, be blameless before men, and trust God has the larger picture in view. We don't need to close doors on those we don't agree with or push people away that have different ideals. Our job is to love and be obedient, even in the hard things. God will shut doors He knows will feel impossible for us to shut on our own. On a boat about half the size of a cruise ship, Noah leads his family into the floating zoo for an undetermined amount of time. The door shuts and his favor will soon carry his family away as everything else he has ever known is washed away.

Cruising is one of my husband and I's favorite ways to vacation. Living in Florida, it doesn't take much time or money to find a last-minute cruise deal, throw some items in a suitcase, and head towards some beautiful island. If we are vacationing by ourselves, we rarely (if ever) get off the boat. The pools are empty, and you don't have to worry about fighting for a nice lounge chair while all the other families head out on the land excursions. This is my husband's *favorite* way to vacation. No plans. No agenda. No timeline. I on the other hand can only sit still for so long until my internal time clock says it's time to do something. Over the years, we have learned to compromise and even jokingly have labeled the "type" of vacation we are going to have before it even starts, so there's no unmet expectations.

Noah and the seven family members who joined him didn't have the choice for what kind of trip they were setting out on. There was no excursion desk or planned stop at some beautiful island. In fact, there was no end of the cruise marked on the calendar at all. God told him how long the heavens would open with rain but left out what forty days and nights of torrential downpours coupled with *"the breaking of the great deep"* would actually look like (Genesis 7:11-12). There was no weather man giving minute-by-minute details or radar to watch on TV. There was no "Spaghetti Model" like we follow incessantly here in Florida during hurricane season.

There was just utter darkness. Utter calamity happening outside their harbor. Zero idea of when it all would end. I can't imagine with the depiction given in Genesis it being a smooth ride for those on board. I'm not going to lie; I get sick to my stomach just thinking about being inside that dark space tossed back and forth with the aroma of every beast you can imagine. They had no crew serving their every whim. They were the crew and the guests were large, smelly, and hungry. It does appear that Noah wouldn't have been the man to turn his nose up at the cruise ship drink package, but I dare say I don't think he would have planned to take enough fruit from the vine to make it last as long as they were on board. It is estimated that Noah and his family were on the ark for over 370 days. Over a year.

Favored. Righteous and blameless. Noah and his family are miraculously safe, yes, but isolated and alone. Alone in what looks much different than paradise and more likely like a pig pen. This reality pales in comparison to the provision and promises or the children's church nursery walls we often think of when we ask God for a favored life. You and I are a product of Noah's obedience. What would heaven have looked like if Noah and his family had decided the cost of obedience was too great, too hard, or too costly? It's easy to get caught up in the miracle of the ark and overlook the cost. What must have been the atmosphere as they all worked hard to keep the ship in running order while Noah's three daughters-in-law would have had their very families left outside the boat? I can't imagine the grief those women endured knowing the children they would one day have would only know one side of their family tree, the top of the tree being their grandfather who, out of obedience, wouldn't allow anyone else onboard. When asked to carry out obedience that leads to the cross, do we expect the cross we bear to be lighter? Do we waver in obedience when it's more difficult than we imagined?

Without much fresh air or personal space for more than a month, I imagine Noah was experiencing a weighty cross in this ark. He probably searched the skies for land every day, but only after God gave him the green light did Noah release two birds to confirm.

> *After forty days Noah opened a window he had made in the ark and <u>sent out a raven, and it kept flying back and forth until the water had dried up from the earth.</u> Then he sent out a dove to see if the water had receded from the surface of the ground. <u>But the dove could find nowhere to perch because there was water over all the surface of the earth; so it returned to Noah in the ark.</u> He reached out his hand and took the dove and brought it back to himself in the ark. He waited seven more days and again sent out the dove from the ark. When the dove returned to him in the evening, there in its beak was a freshly plucked olive leaf! Then Noah knew that the water had receded from the earth. He waited seven more days and sent the dove out again, but this time it did not return to him.*

(Genesis 8:3-12, emphasis added)

In reading this, I skimmed past it at first.

Why did the raven fly back and forth all while the water was in the process of drying up, but the dove he sent out waited until he found dry land to return with an olive branch? Why would God put that in there? I am sometimes blown away at how God works and the very day, as I was preparing to work on this chapter, I stumbled on a message by a man who had the exact same question. Pastor Tim Ross (host of *The Basement Podcast*) years ago preached a message on this. He points out so eloquently that the raven is a carnivorous bird. It feasts on meat. In fact, a quick Google search reveals that ravens enthusiastically love rotting things. This bird had no desire to return because it was probably feasting on the very lives the flood had claimed and yet the dove, as we often see pictured as the Holy Spirit all throughout Scripture, returns once there is evidence of life! This picture is placed there for a reason. This is by no accident. No matter the devastation, God will help us seek out life!

My husband years ago got a tattoo on his arm of a large olive tree. He put it there with the names of myself, our children, and now their spouses hidden in the leaves. The artist named Santana, who so beautifully created this piece of art that now dons his right shoulder, took my husband's idea and actually (as any good artist does) made it more meaningful than even originally intended. You see, my husband, after learning that the olive tree flourishes whether in drought or in excess, wanted this piece to remind himself that no matter the season, he wanted to be a strong, unwavering support for our family. In drought or in abundance, he wanted to stand fast. It wasn't until my husband went back to the same artist to get our son Logan's name changed to red (to stand out as a picture that he was now home and safe) that the artist pointed out something he had hidden in the tattoo we had never seen before. Hidden in the roots of the tree was the name of our God. The source. The roots. The one holding the tree all together. A picture like that of the dove, of life. Even in the face of loss, we are rooted in life.

I'm a very visual learner and love imagery. A simple picture of a landscape, sunrise, or sunset can change my mood immediately. As of recent, sunsets have had the ability to bring a smile but usually at the same time tears. My youngest son loved sunsets. Both of my younger sons took notice of the beauty of a sunset but especially my youngest. He was notorious for wanting to stay at the beach until the sun went down and tucked just beyond the horizon. We saw many sunsets together while casting lines, fishing together side by side. It's hard for me to look at the beautiful sky now without my eyes filling with tears because I can't believe I will never see another one with him here on this side of heaven. Will we have sunsets in heaven? Will we even need them if the heavens are lit by God's glory?

> *The city does not need the sun or the moon to shine on it, for the glory of God gives it light, and the Lamb is its lamp.*

(Revelation 21:23)

What once was such a beautiful reminder of God's faithfulness at the end of another day, for me now stings at what I have lost. Sunsets now make me long for the day we will all be together again and are a painful reminder of another day without him.

Just like sunsets may be hard for me, I wonder if that first rainbow wasn't hard for Noah and his family? Yes, the promise it gave was a beautiful reminder of their safety, but it was also a reminder of what was lost. God has an uncanny ability to take things that were once meant as reminders of death and destruction and turn them into a promise. You don't have to look too hard when out in public before you will see someone wearing a cross necklace, hat, or T-shirt. Bumper stickers and billboards of the local church down the road all display the cross with pride. What once was an archaic torture device built to claim lives now readily displays the hope of life and the promise of heaven. Rainbows are now the same thing for me.

We may not like walking out the favor to carry hard things this side of heaven, but God continues to remind us this is just a small part of eternity. His promises, like rainbows and crosses or doves and olive trees, are set as reminders of the hope that we have in Him and the fact that He still makes good on His promises.

So what do we do when we can't see the rainbow for all the floods we are facing in this life? How do we look for rainbows when all we see is rain? We take the next right step. We remain steadfast. We keep working. We build on the things we know God spoke to us with one swing of the hammer at a time. We work through the stinky mess this life can throw at us, not losing sight of the fact that we don't labor in vain. We labor and work for those we love and those who come behind us (1 Corinthians 9:24-27).

Keep pressing. Keep walking. Keep building. Keep shoveling manure if you have to. It may be hard and feel like the flood is too vast, taking too long to recede, and too heavy a cost, but His promises last forever. When we focus on the promises and not our circumstance, we become capable of carrying unimaginable weight. We grow strong enough to carry out callings that seem improbable and pass on eternal promises that seem impossible. We will impact more than just earthly generations but will help populate the heavens. Let's chase rainbows.

Chapter 6

Grit and Grace

One thing I will never get used to: my phone sending me ads and content based on what I recently mentioned to a friend or even just *thought* about. I'm confident I will always be creeped out by this little black box that's constantly forming opinions and information about me, but one particular night, it actually blew me away. After plenty of research for this chapter, I knew good and well I wanted to call the chapter "Grit and Grace." While lying in bed one night scrolling mindlessly in an attempt to calm my anxious mind, my phone suggested a purchase that caught my eye. A dainty necklace adorned with a beautiful, simple white pearl. The maker of the necklace (Bryan Anthonys) has this beautiful description attached in the packaging:

> "She is unshakable not because she doesn't know pain or failure, but because she always pushes through. Because she always shows up and never gives up. Because she believes anything is possible no matter the odds. And perhaps what makes her beautiful has less to do with what lies upon the surface and more to do with what lies within. She isn't just beautiful because of her appearance. No, she is beautiful because of the way she chooses to live and love. In the way she embraces all of life's experiences – good or bad. In her willingness to bend but never break, and in her courage to believe that the darkness can't hold her as long as she continues to create her own light (Or seek THE light). She is just like a pearl – <u>made from grit but full of grace</u>. She is unstoppable –

she knows it's not what happens, but how she chooses to respond, with perseverance in her mind and passion in her heart."

We will all encounter things in this life that are meant to harm us, hurt us, or discourage us beyond repair. I am forced to face the reality that what was placed inside of my heart that night I lost my son will either take me out or cause something else to grow inside of me.

We can begin to feel that just because it hurts so very much, nothing good could ever come of it. That thing that creeped into our strong shell of a life *will* stop us from moving forward if we aren't literally hell-bent on making something out of it. Nothing beautiful made from my pain will replace what I lost or even how much it hurts, but I refuse to let my loss be greater than my blessing. I was blessed by God to be able to steward the lives of him and his older two brothers. Now I am tasked with also stewarding my sorrow well. It's both.

If we aren't careful, we can decide it has to be either/or. Either *grit* or *grace*. We build walls and thick skin when it comes to how we handle people or situations. Life is hard and has taught us to never back down. In the name of grit or personal boundaries, we push away anyone or anything that challenges us or the status quo we've deemed right in our own hearts. We can be so adamant about protecting ourselves that we rarely let anyone in. The same is true for the other side of the coin.

Under the guise of grace, we put on a beautiful mask and call it mercy. Letting anyone and everyone walk all over us, too shy or too meek and mild to ever take a stand for ourselves. We don't want to let anyone down or have anyone else let us down, so we never set any expectations high enough for anyone to fall from. We let others decide our future and allow someone else to fight for things that should matter to us.

I think our modern-day churches and those of us who call ourselves "Christians" feel the need to swing this pendulum dangerously in one direction or the other, and our world is suffering for it. Some of us have grown so gritty, our world would never come close because just like sandpaper to skin, they know they will get burned by us if they do. We shout about how broken the world is yet feel more compelled to keep our padded church seats warm instead of getting our hands and feet dirty. We can't imagine getting on the ground and making mud pies for the eyes of the blind. We just point fingers and wonder what they did to lose their sight. This world is fighting to find its identity and we are supposed to be the mirror; a beautiful reflection of a strong Savior that flipped tables <u>inside</u> the sanctuary and a tender gentleman that drew a line in the sand and offered a way out to the adulterous woman <u>outside</u> the sanctuary. Both. Grit and grace. Steady but lovely. Strong but compassionate. How are we measuring up? Isn't it interesting that the only people Jesus is known for showing His righteous anger to were the very ones claiming to be the closest to Him?

In this chapter, I want to dig into the life of Esther. This beautiful young woman who had an amazing balance of grit and grace was pushed to determine exactly what she was made of. Unlike the musical pageant *Veggie Tales* version my boys saw while growing up, this was not some fairytale princess story or even some unfair beauty pageant she had no choice of participating in. This was a real girl, with real dreams, real heartache, and her only choice was to endure the life she was given. She was no stranger to loss. She had lost not one but both of her parents at a very young age. Her much older cousin adopted her, and she lived as a refugee in Persia with a secret immigration status. Unbeknownst to her, trouble was brewing in a palace she probably had no illusion of ever even seeing or visiting, much less living in.

> On the seventh day, when the heart of the king was merry with wine, he
> commanded Mehuman, Biztha, Harbona, Bigtha and Abagtha, Zethar and
> Carkas, the seven eunuchs who served in the presence of King Ahasuerus, to
> bring Queen Vashti before the king with her royal crown, in order to show the
> peoples and the princes her beauty, for she was lovely to look at. But Queen
> Vashti refused to come at the king's command delivered by the eunuchs. At this
> the king became enraged, and his anger burned within him.

(Esther 1:10-12)

Queen Vashti refuses to be the king's party favor or prize pony and
declines the nonnegotiable invitation. The depth of this relationship is
truly only skin deep, and he is not only concerned with how people view
his beautiful shiny trophy wife, but more importantly, how they view
him.

> Then Memucan said in the presence of the king and the officials, "Not
> only against the king has Queen Vashti done wrong, but also against all the
> officials and all the peoples who are in all the provinces of King Ahasuerus.
> For the queen's behavior will be made known to all women, causing them to
> look at their husbands with contempt, since they will say, 'King Ahasuerus
> commanded Queen Vashti to be brought before him, and she did not come.'
> this very day the noble women of Persia and Media who have heard of the
> queen's behavior will say the same to all the king's officials, and there will be
> contempt and wrath in plenty. If it please the king, let a royal order go out
> from him, and let it be written among the laws of the Persians and the Medes
> so that it may not be repealed, that Vashti is never again to come before King
> Ahasuerus. And let the king give her royal position to another who is better
> than she.

(Esther 1:16-19)

And just like that, it's out with the old and in with the new. A decree goes out, along with the news of the once famed Vashti, that will not only affect the king's household but everyone in all of Persia.

This is a perfect example of two people who did not know the balance of having both grit and grace. I can't say I blame the queen for taking a stand. The tone of the text leads you to believe he wasn't asking for personal time with her and more so wanted to "display" her beauty to all the men in the room. Who knows what the temperature of that palace truly was. King Ahasuerus (let's call him King Aha from now on) doesn't sound like the kind of king that would have a very long line for a character meet-and-greet if he were a Disney prince.

Both king and queen took a stand that would not only impact their household or generation but generations to come. When we live our lives filled with nothing but grit and the unrealistic expectation to always be right, we impact ourselves *and* all those we come in contact with. Can you imagine the ramifications of what those letters meant to some of the families who received it? The man of the house, no matter his character, morality, or integrity was master. Some of these men (like we are about to see with King Aha) took women as their own from other nations. Now, not only are these wives to meet their husbands every command by law, they are to do so in his language alone, possibly losing not only their self-respect but also the very identity God fashioned them in. Our choices and our decisions spread like seeds in an unkept field. Knowing this is half the battle. *We will grow something.* We get to choose whether or not our actions are slinging out life damaging weeds or life-giving wildflowers.

The King is now on the hunt for his next trophy:

> *Later when King Xerxes' fury had subsided, he remembered Vashti and what she had done and what he had decreed about her. Then the king's personal attendants proposed, "Let a search be made for beautiful young virgins for the king. Let the king appoint commissioners in every province of his realm to bring all these beautiful young women into the harem at the citadel of Susa. Let them be placed under the care of Hegai, the king's eunuch, who is in charge of the women; and let beauty treatments be given to them. Then let the young woman who pleases the king be queen instead of Vashti." This advice appealed to the king, and he followed it.*

(Esther 2:1-4)

Brought, sought out, gathered. No matter the version of the Bible you read, those terms are more chilling than endearing. Nowhere does it say these women lined up, volunteered, or applied. These were young virgin women taken without a promise and placed into the hands of a caregiver they did not choose.

I think as a little girl, hearing this story with my pageant-tinted glasses on, the idea of being placed in a castle sounded like a fairytale. Add in the free beauty treatments, and I'm picturing a nineties *Clueless*-themed slumber party with all my bffs. Often it's not even what the scriptures say but our vain imaginations—what we have been taught or at least what we have taken to heart while tossing out the rest—that truly sticks with us. We want to glaze over the truth of the story and instead picture some renaissance-esque painting, colors flowing, smiles highlighted, forgetting to actually tally up the cost of the lives depicted on canvas. The cost of favor.

Growing up in the South, I had quite the mixed bag of experiences and childhood memories. I could climb trees with the best of them, hook a worm, and tear through the woods slinging mud on any ATV you threw at me. I also learned to shoot very well, earning the name Dead-Eye Dee from a very early age after outshooting most of the boys in the family. *Toot Toot!* (You hear that? That's me tooting my own horn.) To date, I'm pretty sure I am the only fourth grader in all of history to bring her prized hunt to school for Show-and-Tell. Getting my mom to say yes to that one took some convincing on my dad and I's part, and I'm pretty sure poor Mrs. Fitzgerald about had a heart attack when my little gloved hands (safety first) pulled out an armadillo to show to the class.

Although I loved playing in the dirt, slinging a softball, and running the neighborhood, I also had a very girly side. I had the *Barbie* Dream House and the *My Little Pony* barn complete with all the fixings, and I loved to dress up. My mom would roll my hair with big, thick, pink curlers every Saturday night so that my poofy church dress would rival my poofy bouffant (the higher the hair, the closer to God). The former taught me grit and the latter taught me grace.

All that grit and grace had to be on display somehow, and at the ripe old age of three, my little gritty southern soul hit the stage for my very first beauty pageant: Miss Continental. I loved every minute of it. 'Til I didn't.

I loved playing dress-up and prancing out my talent like some magical knock-off princess until I got to the age to realize there was a lot behind the scenes that made me feel very uncomfortable. It wasn't all about talent, and it wasn't all about poise. It was about favor. Favored beauty. Favored sponsors. Favored parents. Favored influence.

I'll never forget one of my last pageants. There was this beautiful girl that was for sure the front runner. She had an entire beauty team around her (hair, makeup, modeling coach). She was blonde, bright-eyed, and had the most amazing blue Cinderella dress. With the sweetest southern drawl, she answered the judges' questions so perfectly and eloquently. She looked every bit the part of beauty and grace as she stood under those hot lights in that historic old theater, but backstage was a totally different story.

Her cute twangy accent quickly dissipated as she barked orders at her mother and beauty team. As other girls performed their talent, she laughed and rolled her eyes and made fun of each and every one of us. To be sure, she definitely wasn't in the running for Miss Congeniality, but at the end of the day, the winning crown was the perfect final touch to that beautiful dress as she waved to the crowd saying, "thank y'all." It was one of the first times in my life I began to understand that what everyone displays on the outside has little if anything to do with what they are really made of on the inside. I had to decide which one was more important to me—what people saw or who I was.

About two years ago for our twenty-fifth wedding anniversary, we bought a 1969 VW Bug, reminiscent of the first car my husband had while we were dating. When we got the car, we dreamed about how we would cruise in it on sunny days and where it would take us. We knew we were only a few years away from a quickly approaching empty nest. We went and picked it out together with our youngest son, and the memory of them driving that car home together is one I'll never forget.

After the loss of our son, that car sat for quite a while. It sat for almost a year. Driving in it didn't feel the same. The wind that blew in our hair now felt like a slap in the face, and we truly debated on selling it. In the end (at least to date), the car is still ours, and if you live anywhere near us, you've probably seen my husband tooling around in his baby blue bug. It's just a thing, an item, a car. I know that, but for us, it's a sign of hope and promise and love. A few months back, my husband and I on a squirrely Saturday morning decided to check out a local car auction. We know *nothing* about buying/selling cars (as was evident when we realized we were bidding against ourselves) but we were very intrigued to just check it out. Here we sat on the back seat of the bleachers watching the callers call and the bidders bid, all of them placing a value on a specific vehicle. Some of the buyers kicked the tires, inspected for dents, and checked to see what was under the hood.

With that imagery in mind, I now read the story of Esther. A lot less fairytale and with a whole lot more car auction vibes, I picture the king's "commissioners" lining up, taking numbers, and inspecting the goods with no concern about each girl's personal story. Kicking the tires and comparing each face with the previous queen to see how they would line up, each commissioner vied to make a name for themselves by finding the best "purchase" (although no price was paid for these women). There was no sentimental weight placed on these souls. No concept that one of these women may possibly be a sign of hope, promise, or love. There was no real test of their character or identity. They were weighed by outside beauty and physical purity only and not at all what they would represent. The attendants (the car lot owner) commands the eunuch (the mechanic) to spruce up the goods so King Aha could take his pick and put a ring on it when he decided he was good and ready.

> So it was, when the king's command and decree were heard, and when many young women were <u>gathered</u> at Shushan the citadel, under the custody of Hegai, that Esther also was <u>taken</u> to the king's palace, into the care of Hegai, the custodian of the women. Now the young woman pleased him, and

she obtained his <u>favor</u>; so he readily gave beauty preparations to her, besides her allowance. Then seven choice maid servants were provided for her from the king's palace, and he moved her and her maid servants to the best place in the house of the women.

(Esther 2:8-9, emphasis added)

Born of foreign blood and raised by her foreign older cousin who himself had been captured and brought to this land unwillingly, Esther never considers fleeing. Her people had been taken and misplaced. She was at the same mercy to the king that all of her people were and had been before her. The generations before her had all suffered the same fate, and it was all she had ever known. She's taken into the custody of Hegai the Eunuch and quickly shows she is not just a one-trick pony filled with the grit to fight to make it this far; she is also bubbling over with grace. How do I know that? She found "favor" in his eyes and pleased him and all who saw her. Before we get too much further along and you think any less of this poor girl who could have landed a book deal on her tragic story about being "taken by the king," the favor she found from Hegai would have had to have been totally pure in nature. Filled with grace, kindness, personality, and a good temperament, she wins his favor.

How would one deduce this? Eunuchs (specifically those in charge of women in those times), were most often a slave themselves, taken and considered property of the king and were castrated to make sure there was no misconduct. If you're a man reading this, that may have woken you up. This eunuch knew what it was like to be taken and have someone else run his life; this beautiful, favored girl garners his attention, and I believe it had to have been for one reason only. God was with her. Yes, she was formed on the streets of hard things, a stolen/displaced bloodline that formed her, but she also had grace oozing from her. That grace was the grace of God.

> *Esther had not revealed her people or family, for Mordecai had charged her not to reveal it. And every day Mordecai paced in front of the court of the women's quarters, to learn of Esther's welfare and what was happening to her.*

(Esther 2:10-11)

These verses are not only a picture of how unstable the situation is for Esther as a young girl with a hidden nationality in a house that gives her no worth or authority, but also a glimpse at the worry and concern her now-father (cousin) Mordecai is processing. My heart aches as I can see him pacing back and forth, back and forth, every day, just hoping to catch a glimpse of his beautiful, adopted daughter over whom he was given charge. Totally out of his control but refusing not to be as present as possible, this man does everything he can to continue to be there for Esther and remind her of who she is.

As a mama, I want there to be more. I want there to be some grand miracle or angel to swoop in to make sure she is safe. I want to see the heavens pour out and take away his worry for his sweet daughter, but all he can do is keep taking another step. And another. And another. And another. Sometimes we will see grand miracles, and other times we will have to walk alongside our kids, outside the gate, yelling from the other side, reminding them of who they are as they walk through really hard things, figuring out their own way to their own God.

> *Each young woman's turn came to go in to King Ahasuerus after she had completed twelve months' preparation, according to the regulations for the women, for thus were the days of their preparation apportioned: six months*

with oil of myrrh, and six months with perfumes and preparations for beautifying women. Thus prepared, each young woman went to the king, and she was given whatever she desired to take with her from the women's quarters to the king's palace. In the evening she went, and in the morning she returned to the second house of the women, to the custody of Shaashgaz, the king's eunuch who kept the concubines. She would not go in to the king again unless the king delighted in her and called for her by name.

(Esther 2:12-14)

Tires kicked and all hoods looked under, the women were sent to King Aha one by one. Unlike the talent show I mentioned earlier in the chapter, I highly doubt the King was looking for who could twirl the best baton or hit the highest note. After their encounter with the king, these women were taken from the custody of one eunuch, Hegai (the virgins), to another's custody: Shaashgaz (concubines). Ushered from one house to the next all dependent upon a task they never requested to perform with the decision on where they would reside totally dependent on the fleeting passions of a king. True romance.

Now when the turn came for Esther the daughter of Abihail the uncle of Mordecai, who had taken her as his daughter, to go in to the king, she requested nothing but what Hegai the king's eunuch, the custodian of the women, advised. And Esther obtained favor in the sight of all who saw her.

So Esther was taken to King Ahasuerus, into his royal palace, in the tenth month, which is the month of Tebeth, in the seventh year of his reign. The king loved Esther more than all the other women, and she obtained grace and _favor_ in his sight more than all the virgins; so he set the royal crown upon her head and made her queen instead of Vashti. Then the king made a great feast, the Feast of Esther, for all his officials and servants; and he proclaimed a holiday in the provinces and gave gifts according to the generosity of a king.

(Esther 2:15-18, emphasis added)

I do wonder what the other women took as they were called to the king. Was it like a show-and-tell where they all brought a piece of who they were? Or was it more of them bringing their belongings hoping they would be moving right away to the big palace? Who knows, but her friend Hegai knows the king well. He tells her to request nothing but what he suggests. He helps her know the way to the king's heart (although I'm not sure the depth of it). Here, Hegai, a man who has had everything taken from him, is found helping another in his same shoes. Sometimes powerlessness and loss make people bitter and angry; sometimes it makes them compassionate and kind and gives purpose. I hope the same can be said about me as I walk through loss. How we walk through suffering is not picked for us. We get to choose.

Thinking back to the strawberry festival I mentioned in a previous chapter, there's one spot we as a family somehow always, without fail, end up: the dunk tank. There in the same back corner every year is a clown that sits high up on a little beam over a massive water tank. He has the most recognizable, high-pitched scratchy voice that slings out insults to the crowd as they walk by. You would think this wouldn't be the place to be, but call it cringy curiosity, our family gets sucked in every time.

Everyone knows the act. Everyone knows the more he can get under your skin with his insults and jabs, the more money you will throw down in order to try to sink him into the tank. Time after time, like a *National Geographic* documentary, he picks the right stray from the herd unknowingly passing by who can't stand for him to tease their outfit, their date, or their mama and out comes the cash. Shouting in his screechy voice, "High and dry am I!"

The real kicker though is even if you get a lucky shot and you sink him, he never bats an eyelash. He just declares, "Winner winner, chicken dinner!" and starts up on his next prey. I don't know if it's a nod, acknowledging you paid for his next meal, or just his way to rub salt in the wound, but he has little time to waste. He's on to the next. Dunking the clown might feel like "winning," but the game is designed for it. The money is in the hands of the clown regardless.

And the crown still perpetuated the same faulty system.

I feel like "winning" the crown here must have felt little to any different than sinking that rodeo clown. Her identity is still unknown. She is still just another pawn in the castle. There was always someone else right behind her, ready to take any "prize" or crown that I'm sure carried little weight when compared to her freedom.

Often when hearing the story of Esther, we quickly go from beauty treatments to saving a nation with little regard to what it took and what she had to endure to get to that point. When the king's right-hand man Haman's pride gets checked by Esther's legal guardian (unbeknownst to Haman and King Aha), and he finds out Mordecai is a Jew, Haman decides to plan a genocide of all her people. Many will declare the "favor" over Esther during this scene as a miracle, but in actuality, it was once again God making *all things work together for good* despite the horrific circumstances it took to obtain (Romans 8:28). Haman was of Amalekite descent. King Saul—years prior to Esther's reign—had been instructed by God to destroy this enemy of the Lord due to their horrific acts on the Jewish people six centuries earlier. Saul disobeyed. Saul's disobedience to carry out God's command now impacted generations and was placed directly into Esther's lap. She had to bear the weight of his decision, a decision she didn't ask for nor had been made by her. God's favor granted her the strength to endure and save a nation, but this is just more proof that our obedience or disobedience does not just affect us. It will continue to affect the generations in front of us (and behind).

Filled with fear about approaching a throne deemed a death sentence without an invitation, Esther's father figure knew it was time to go from "worried prayer warrior outside the gate" to "faith-fueled mentor," challenging what he knows she is made of:

> *Then Esther spoke to Hathach, and gave him a command for Mordecai: "All the king's servants and the people of the king's provinces know that any man or woman who goes into the inner court to the king, who has not been called, he has but one law: put all to death, except the one to whom the king holds out the golden scepter, that he may live. Yet I myself have not been called to go in to the king these thirty days." So they told Mordecai Esther's words.*
>
> *And Mordecai told them to answer Esther: "Do not think in your heart that you will escape in the king's palace any more than all the other Jews. For if you remain completely silent at this time, relief and deliverance will arise for the Jews from another place, but you and your father's house will perish.*
>
> *Yet who knows whether you have come to the kingdom for such a time as this?"*

(Esther 4:10-14, emphasis added)

For such a time as this. For such a time as this you were placed here on this earth. For such a time as this, you have faced insurmountable odds and obstacles. For such a time as this, you know what is inside of you and who God created you to be. For such a time as this, it matters not what the generation did before you or the six generations prior that didn't have the strength to rise up and stand up for their family and their future. For such a time as this, miracles happen but sometimes on the back of war-torn/tear-stained humans looking for the next right step. For such a time as this He has given you the favor to carry the weight whether you believe it or not.

> *Then Esther told them to reply to Mordecai: "Go, gather all the Jews who are present in Shushan, and fast for me; neither eat nor drink for three days, night or day. My maids and I will fast likewise. And so I will go to the king, which is against the law; <u>and if I perish, I perish</u>!"*

(Esther 4:16, emphasis added)

Esther's focus changed quickly from herself to those around her. She led from a position and not a title, with a posture and not a placement. She won the hearts of those around her with her grace, yet when push came to shove, refused to back down from what she knew was right, even if it meant her life.

We have no choice but to face many of the circumstances we are given in this life, but we do have the choice of whether or not we will face them with strength and courage. It matters. If I perish, I perish, but I will do so fighting hell to do what's right.

Chapter 7

Giant Slayer

Raising three boys was and will forever be one of my greatest treasures this side of heaven. That being said, there were days it was hard. I learned to hold loosely to any trinket or breakable item I would dare bring into the house and would try to not cringe or wince when I heard that crashing sound followed by a very loud "sorry."

We tried so hard in an ever-changing world and culture to raise young men tender enough to chase the heart of God and yet strong enough to face giants. Pockets filled with acorns and rocks but also feathers and flowers was a good indication on laundry day that they were prayerfully on the right track. I am forever proud of the fight they have inside to stand up for what is right but also the softness to stand up for others, including themselves.

I'll never forget one particular day seeing this play out in full force on the playground. The boys were running and playing with a few other kids, and the game of choice was tag. Everyone was getting along just fine until this one particular boy showed up. He was rough. He was unkind. He was the playground bully. This wasn't my local neighborhood play place to bring the boys, and as I looked around, I noticed I was the only parent in sight. My Mama Bear ears were perked up as I heard him shouting at some of the kids and saw him targeting some of the younger ones, including my youngest, Logan.

After seeing my son take a good hard shove to the ground, I stood to my feet ready to step in. I asked him firmly to keep his hands to himself as he glared at me like, "What are you going to do about it?" At this moment, I realized that I was about to do one of two things: Embarrass my kids by losing my mind on this boy, or get arrested for endangering a minor.

I quickly changed my course and went with Plan C. I called over my oldest son. At about the same age and height, I asked my eldest to keep an eye on his younger brother and to let that other boy know the little kid he was messing with had two older brothers out there on the playground.

The bully laid low for a little while, and I thought the issue had been diffused until my older two got just far enough away for the bully to take his shot. Logan was down on the ground again. I jumped to my feet but paused as his older brothers ran towards the scene of the crime; my youngest son came up filled with rage and fists full of mulch and dirt, slinging them right into that bully's eyes, shouting "Keep your hands off of me! Don't you touch me again. Do you hear me? Leave me alone!"

I kid you not, that big/little boy that was taunting the playground went running crying away from the park, and it felt like the end of a classic eighties movie where the victor is hoisted on the shoulders and declared champion. My youngest cub had stood up for himself that day and claimed his turf. It changed the entire tone not just for him but for those on the playground that day.

"Small fry," "fun size," and "short stuff" were just a few of the names my youngest wore with pride as a young boy growing up. One of his favorite t-shirts when he was little was a *Star Wars* Yoda shirt with the phrase "Judge me by my size, do you?" The smallest in his class from year to year, he often had to fight the stigma and the lie that what was on the outside dictated the strength on the inside. He was heaven-bent on proving the opposite.

The youngest, the smallest, and the least qualified, we find our next favored friend tending to the family's farm by herding and protecting the sheep of the field. Any guesses? The once-famed judge, now-prophet Samuel is on the hunt for the next king to satiate the desires of an easily displeased Israelite people. King Saul had disobeyed the commands of God and was going to be replaced. God had given the people the king they had wanted, and now He decided to give them the king they need in 1 Samuel 16:10.

I know a lot of people put weight into the Birth Order Theory, and I myself think there must be something to it. Siblings for as long as the world has turned 'round have claimed the youngest gets away with everything and is usually spoiled or given special treatment (Joseph has entered the chat). I myself (being the youngest) can neither confirm nor deny and tend to think I wasn't given special treatment. I was just that amazing of a kid...but I digress.

Here in the first verses, we sort of see the exact opposite. Jesse thinks so little of the youngest son he has in the fields that he doesn't even have him come up to the house when this man of God comes looking for who could be dubbed next to lead His people. He wasn't just picked last to be looked at by his dad. He wasn't even invited to the anointing party. Have you ever thought about what that would have done to the heart of a young man? When God said, *"Man looks at the outward appearance, but God looks at the heart,"* I don't think He was only looking for purity of heart but also strength and humility; a good work ethic and someone He could trust with really hard things (1 Samuel 16:7). God knew good and well what David would have to face in the years ahead before he claimed his throne and his title. God knew He needed a man who found his confidence in who He said He was and not in what others thought. And so David returns to the field.

It blows my mind that after such a high calling is placed on David's future—complete with an oil bath in front of his older brothers and father—*he returns to the fields*. Unlike our friend Joseph, we don't see David touting what the prophet said, treating his brothers differently, or asking those around him, "Do you know who I am?" No. We see the same servant that will one day lead a nation head back to his post to serve his family and lead sheep. Too often if we aren't careful, we can decide our title and calling are more important than the current thing God has placed in our hands to steward. With eyes focused on platforms instead of character, we step into roles prematurely. We will never be able to lead healthy nations if we feel too high and mighty to nurture sheep.

One of the psalms that has been nearest and dearest to mine and my husband's heart this past year has been Psalms 23. Penned by this shepherd boy-turned king, he doesn't write from a position of power but from a posture of purpose. He writes of himself not as a great and mighty leader but as the one being led.

Our delayed callings and assignments are not for nothing. They are seasons of preparation and realignment. Are we doing the work in the unseen seasons to be bold enough to not only walk into the presence of our enemies but be Spirit led enough to soothe their souls?

> *Now the Spirit of the LORD had departed from Saul, and an evil spirit from the LORD tormented him. Saul's attendants said to him, "See, an evil spirit from God is tormenting you. Let our lord command his servants here to search*

for someone who can play the lyre. He will play when the evil spirit from God comes on you, and you will feel better."

[...]

Whenever the spirit from God came on Saul, David would take up his lyre and play. Then relief would come to Saul; he would feel better, and the evil spirit would leave him.

1 Samuel 16:14-23

Only with the currency of grace on display in heaven could the very martyrs killed for sharing their faith be the same ones to welcome their captors home, and here we see David soothing what will soon be his enemy. Sometimes God will ask us to sling stones at our enemies, and other times, He will have us serving selflessly alongside someone who may one day turn on us and become our enemy, using weapons they once offered us in battle against us. God's grace and mercy is far different from our own.

Picked over as a boy and now calling delayed, David steps into the household of the king not in the role the prophet or as what his anointing gave him but as a servant. As an armor-bearer and basically a living and breathing Alexa told to play songs on demand; he is called in to soothe the nerves and demons of the very man who was supposed to be leading the nation.

God sometimes allows us into the hidden spaces and places of a calling years before we step into it. We sometimes even throw up our hands and ask God why we are in the waiting room of our future while those in charge are not leading well, perhaps even fully incapacitated by their own demons. The highest man in the land needed help from a shepherd boy not because of what he knew or even because of his talents but because of what and who he had within him. This won't be the first time he will need the giant living inside this boy.

Summer days at our house full of boys were filled with wiffle ball games in the street, backyard campouts, and a game the boys created that was a very dangerous version of tag on wheels called Rip-Stick Wars. They loved playing outside, but I think my youngest may have loved it the most. We had the amazing privilege of living in an incredible neighborhood for about four years during his childhood, and it is true that good people make all the difference.

There was a whole mess of boys in that little quiet subdivision, and they made the most of every day. Bouncing from house to house in search of who had the best snacks, they often ended up at the house next door. Our next-door neighbor became like a bonus grandmother to anyone who would let her. She was the neighborhood watch, the town crier, and HOA all rolled into one. A three-time cancer survivor with a strong New York accent, you never had to wonder where you stood with her, and we loved her. We loved her dearly! (She is now in heaven with our son, and I can only imagine the fun those two are having together.)

Logan and his friends were always up to something (building a fort, whittling swords that ended with stitches, etc.). This particular day, I got a phone call and saw on the caller ID the name "Lila," our next-door neighbor. She said, "Now I'm not one to pry..." (which still makes me laugh because that was literally what she was best known for) "...but you may want to check on your youngest son. I think he's building the world's largest slingshot."

Sure enough, I kid you not, I walk outside to see the branch my husband had just recently cut down, now trimmed up in the ground with large bungee cords attached ready to fire. As to not discourage the little heart of the one who had just created this weapon of mass destruction, I strongly gave some ground rules, turned it away from the neighbors' windows, and asked him to please shoot tennis balls instead of rocks. I wonder if David's mom ever had such stories.

Out in the fields, making the most of every day and creating his own fun, I picture David whittling that slingshot, making a game of target practice and honing his skill. If you are a mama of little ones reading this book, I challenge you to let them try hard things. You may never know the giant they are preparing to slay in the future. They will need bravery, a backbone, and the skill to face all the giants the world throws at them. With the encouragement to do hard things and our introduction to the One that will give them the strength to fight all hell throws at them, they just may surprise us. They may not only lead us one day, but they may show us who our trust truly lies in.

Still anointed and still serving, we find David pulling double-duty, going back and forth between keeping the king's demons at bay and tending to his father's sheep. Still the youngest and the lowest man on the family totem pole, David's father asks him to take some extra food up to the military camp where his three eldest brothers are serving and report back on their well-being. He shows up expecting to see his three older brothers fighting the enemy but instead sees an entire army cowering not only to the giant in front of them but by their lack of belief in a God who was with them.

We don't usually see the giants that block our victories as "favor." We see them as sure defeat, but it is not the giant who defeats us but our own lack of trust in the one capable of helping us fight them. David knew he had nothing to lose. He wasn't scared of death. He trusted the promise spoken over his life and knew the kingdom he fought for was more powerful than any earthly kingdom he would potentially acquire.

> *David asked the men standing near him, "What will be done for the man who kills this Philistine and removes this disgrace from Israel? Who is this uncircumcised Philistine that he should defy the armies of the living God?" They repeated to him what they had been saying and told him, "This is what will be done for the man who kills him." When Eliab, David's oldest brother, heard him speaking with the men, he burned with anger at him and asked, "Why have you come down here? And with whom did you leave those few sheep in the wilderness? I know how conceited you are and how wicked your heart is; you came down only to watch the battle." "Now what have I done?" said David. "Can't I even speak?" He then turned away to someone else and brought up the same matter, and the men answered him as before. What David said was overheard and reported to Saul, and Saul sent for him.*

(1 Samuel 17:26-31)

"Go back to your sheep."

"Remember who you are."

David's brother (call it jealousy, embarrassment, or fear) wants to remind his little brother that regardless of what he was told he would become, he was far from it at the moment. Saul, only knowing David as his soul-soother up to this point, thinks he could never defeat such an enemy and probably wasn't even concerned with who he had potentially betrothed his daughter to because the odds of this boy fighting a well-trained killer were more than unlikely. David's assurance lies in what he had already seen God help him do while no one else was around. On his own, he had defeated lions and bears while tending to his sheep and trusted that if his God was with him then, he would surely be with him now.

The battles we fight when no one is around to cheer us on or discourage us are where we actually find out what we are and who we truly believe in. Don't despise the desert or the dark where you feel isolated and alone. The sheep you are tending to are training ground.

> *Then Saul dressed David in his own tunic. He put a coat of armor on him and a bronze helmet on his head. David fastened on his sword over the tunic and tried walking around, because he was not used to them. "I cannot go in these," he said to Saul, "because I am not used to them." So he took them off. Then he took his staff in his hand, chose five smooth stones from the stream, put them in the pouch of his shepherd's bag and, with his sling in his hand, approached the Philistine.*

(1 Samuel 17:38-40)

Remember when I said, as a young girl, I was asked to model the Armor of God in front of my church camp? It was uncomfortable and not made to size. As I stood in the front of that small kids camp chapel in the mountains of Georgia, I did my best to straighten my posture and fill out that costume made for someone else. Here, David in much the same way is given the costume of a fighter knowing good and well the armor he held within was more powerful than any part he could play in another man's shadow. Saul thought he was trying to prepare a young man for battle against a foreign enemy. He didn't realize the pebble that was about to take out the enemy would also cause a ripple, changing his own future as well.

> *David said to the Philistine, "You come against me with sword and spear and javelin, but I come against you in the name of the LORD Almighty, the*

*God of the armies of Israel, whom you have defied. This day the L*ORD *will deliver you into my hands, and I'll strike you down and cut off your head. This very day I will give the carcasses of the Philistine army to the birds and the wild animals, and the whole world will know that there is a God in Israel. All those gathered here will know that it is not by sword or spear that the L*ORD *saves; for the battle is the L*ORD*'s, and he will give all of you into our hands."*

As the Philistine moved closer to attack him, David ran quickly toward the battle line to meet him. Reaching into his bag and taking out a stone, he slung it and struck the Philistine on the forehead. The stone sank into his forehead, and he fell facedown on the ground.

(1 Samuel 17:45-49)

As I read this with fresh eyes, I'm taken back by the fact that the giant fell *toward* David. Toward the enemy. Toward the ones he had been taunting. I want to give David credit here because he obviously was a skilled marksman with his slingshot, but have you ever hit something from the front and *not* watched it fall back? Surely physics alone would dictate otherwise, and yet we find this giant falling forward, bowing before not only David, but the God he had been taunting. God didn't need David's strength, bravery, or skill to take down the giant. He chose to use him. He knew He could trust the boy who trusted Him.

David wasn't fighting alone, and neither are you. Your giant and my giant may be vastly different, but the God who fights for us need not be. He sees the battles raging in front of us. He knows the enemy well. He knows we aren't fighting just for things here on earth but for things that will echo in eternity, and all He requires of us is to take the next right step. The next step towards our enemy. Face on. Possibly fearing nothing or maybe full of fear but faithfully stepping just the same.

Giants meant to kill us can often make others take notice. When we walk according to the size of God we have on the inside instead of the size man has made us on the outside, others will notice and be drawn to the why.

When the men were returning home after David had killed the Philistine, the women came out from all the towns of Israel to meet King Saul with singing and dancing, with joyful songs and with timbrels and lyres. As they danced, they sang:

"Saul has slain his thousands,
and David his tens of thousands."

Saul was very angry; this refrain displeased him greatly. "They have credited David with tens of thousands," he thought, "but me with only thousands. What more can he get but the kingdom?" And from that time on Saul kept a close eye on David.

(1 Samuel 18:6-9)

Others are watching. Even being in ministry for so long and having others watch us under what felt like a microscope for years has been nothing like what we have experienced as a family this past year(s).

Levi Lusko in his book, *Through the Eyes of a Lion*, says it like this: "Pain gives you a microphone you never asked for. People will lean in to see if the God you really believe in is real even now in your pain." The giant I now face is grief. I am riddled with the thoughts of what I wanted or expected never happening the way they should have in a perfect world. I have seen God move mountains before, heal before, and protect before, but now I am faced with a new giant. The giant of suffering well.

The others now pale in comparison to this new giant, and others are watching. Leaning in to see what I will do now with this faith God birthed inside of me at such a young age. I often wonder if I'll be able to keep choosing to stand, to believe, to fight, to hope. My expectations and my reality are grossly different, but I trust (most days) the one who in the past has helped me fight my battles. The character of God does not change when He doesn't answer the way I thought He would or meet my demands—a reality I will always have to remind myself of when I'm disappointed. He is still good, and if I believe that, I can believe the promises He spoke over my life, my husband's life, and my children's lives, knowing it isn't for an earthly kingdom but for a heavenly one. The battle is great and far bigger than any I have ever been given insight to in the past. Will the Kingdom that lasts forever look different because of the God inside of me?

David goes from slaying giants to hiding in the rock as he flees for safety from the man he once served. His crown and his kingdom weren't handed to him on a silver platter, and often things that matter and last aren't won easily either.

You may be similar. You may have had moments of victory and now find yourself hiding, licking your wounds, wondering, "Where is God?" Maybe even like me, you've seen giants fall and now wonder where the God is that went to battle for you. You may have thought that to be in favor with the Lord exempts you and your family from hard things.

I can list seventy-three psalms our great giant slayer wrote and most suggest otherwise. We will all face hard things. No one this side of the Garden of Eden is spared, but how we respond will dictate the future of not only those here but for all eternity. I've never leaned so much on the book of Psalms like I have this past year. The Psalms written while hiding in the rock resonate with me so much more than his entire encounter and victory with the Philistine. Some of David's battles were of his own doing, but some he had no control over. The only difference between his battles, sin, and losses were what he did on the other side of them. He fought to find God in them. He didn't retreat when giant after giant came closer to attack him. He stood firm on the promise that he was anointed by God to be a ruler in this kingdom and the next.

David is the only one called the man after God's own heart. Not because he was perfect, never sinned, or never faced hard things but because he always turned to the one that would make it matter for eternity. You aren't less-than or unqualified no matter if you are a shepherd or a king.

The Lord is my shepherd; I shall not want. He maketh me to lie down in green pastures: he leadeth me beside the still waters. He restoreth my soul: he leadeth me in the paths of righteousness for his name's sake. Yea, though I walk through the valley of the shadow of death, I will fear no evil: for thou art with me; thy rod and thy staff they comfort me. Thou preparest a table before me in the presence of mine enemies: thou anointest my head with oil; my cup runneth over. Surely goodness and mercy shall follow me all the days of my life: and I will dwell in the house of the Lord for ever.

Psalm 23 KJV

Chapter 8

Taking Back Egypt

"I have brand-new puppies, and I think coming to cuddle and spend a little time with them would be good therapy for you," my sweet and trusted friend Susie said. Only three weeks had passed since we had lost our son when I got that message from Susie about her new brood of goldendoodles.

I was desperate for anything that would give me any kind of reprieve. I barely remember most of what happened those first few days and weeks. I just remember feeling like I didn't know if I would make it. Every day felt like I had some new uncontrollable pain searing through every cell of my body. Trauma and grief do more than form tears that fall by the buckets. They wreak havoc on everything you've trusted, including your own senses.

Those first few weeks, I almost felt as if I were floating in a world of pain outside myself. Even in rooms filled to the brim with people who loved our family and our son, I felt alone and I was desperate to make the pain stop. It was in one of my darkest moments I got this sweet message about a new litter of puppies. Dear friends of ours that lead a beautiful church down in the center of Ybor City, one of the toughest communities in all the Tampa Bay area, also breed gorgeous goldendoodle puppies.

As I sat letting the tears fall while cuddling each and every one of those little furballs, it felt good to just hold something so tender while feeling so vulnerable and fragile myself.

Fully aware that the demands and cost of their beautiful special-needs daughter may outlast their lifetime and without any inheritance two ministers could garner up, our friends began this side business of breeding goldendoodles to provide for her future. Looking back, it was quite possibly the first glimpse of God trying to show me someone who had faced insurmountable obstacles but was fighting to keep taking the next right step. The puppy kisses didn't hurt either.

About six weeks later, I got another message from Susie letting me know the puppies were getting big. If I wanted one more "therapy" session, I had better come soon because they were all getting ready to go to their forever homes. Still weak from grief and trauma and not trusting myself enough behind the wheel to drive, my dear friend Sharon drove me across town with the prescription of puppy kisses and strict instructions not to try to bring one home with me. Joking all the way there that I may try to sneak one out, I was literally speechless as Susie handed me a card that said, "Pick out your puppy. God told me you needed one."

"But I can't afford them," I said. "We already have a four-year-old dog, and my husband will never say yes to another." She had already reached out to my husband, and he had wholeheartedly agreed to accept this thoughtful and sacrificial gift. I tearfully and carefully picked out the one puppy who seemed to need my cuddles as much as I needed hers. I needed something to nurture. I needed something to love. I needed something to get me out of bed in the morning, and the rowdy skittish puppy we named Nala was just the thing.

I've had dogs ever since I can remember. From German shepherds to puggles, hybrids to rescues, we've run the gamut with different breeds. With that in mind, if I hadn't seen the beautiful environment Nala was born in or known her since she was a tiny pup, I would have thought for sure she had lived a life with sleepless nights on the streets in a cruel world. As a rescue, her skittish behavior would make total sense, and I would be willing to bet my life she had been beaten with a trash bag, vacuum cleaner, mailbox, or water faucet. In Nala's world, if it moves or makes a noise of *any* kind, it's scary. This played out in grandeur on one day in particular.

Our pool has two little waterfalls that shoot up and keep the water flowing throughout the day. Nala, being on her morning lizard hunt, happened to be on the other side of the pool when the pool pump kicked on and started our miniature water show. With water to the left of her and a wind-blown hammock to the right, she was paralyzed in fear. I tried everything to coax her. Treats. *Nope*. Cheers. *Nada*. Petting and tugging. *Forget about it*. She wasn't budging. She was immobile, trembling and stricken with fear.

As I picked up and carried my almost sixty-pound pup, hoping she wouldn't wiggle us both into the pool, it hit me how much we were alike. Frozen. Stricken with fear. Untrusting of the master. I have never allowed anything to harm her, yet she desperately struggles to trust the environment, even when I try to convince her it's safe. I see a lot of myself in her.

My fears feel more real than hers as my world has proven to be a scary place. I find myself wobbling left and right wondering if more "favor" or protection are found one way or the other. If rain falls on the just and the unjust, the favored and unfavored, His people and those that claim they aren't, how will I find enough strength to keep fighting and finish well? How do I ever rebuild trust?

Not only did the chosen people of the Bible have the same questions and fears, but their Hebrews 11 hero of the faith leader, Moses, did as well. My church experiences have leaned more on the *miracles* when teaching the crazy stories donning the pages of Exodus instead of the doubts, questions, and fears, but they are mixed in all the same. Moses had the guts to ask God the most authentic, bold, and vulnerable questions like *who, what, where, when,* and *why*? Moses may have indeed been a better journalist or author than God-fearing prophet (at the beginning). Long before he encounters the burning bush and stacks his arguments against God's plan, his mother stands up to the government. Pharaoh, not liking the growing number of little Hebrew boys who would one day turn into men, decides to take the first stand against the very people God calls His favored. With all the healthy baby boys sentenced to death before they even have a chance at life, Jochebed defies the law in Exodus 2:2-10 (technically obeying by throwing her son in the Nile, but in a basket), and her brazen attempt to save her son's life will change the course of a nation.

I've read these verses for years. Ever since I was a little girl, I pictured what it must have felt like to place that beautiful healthy boy in a basket. I've always thought I would have rather died in defiance than trusted the outcome of my own DIY baby ark. What hits me harder now is knowing that although God had provided a way for him to be safe in the basket and found (like a little lost puppy) by the Pharaoh's daughter who would raise him, His real mother (Jochebed) would have to let him go not just once but twice. Which would have been harder? Placing him in a basket thinking he may surely die, or placing him in a palace and the hands of a king known for celebrating the death of the innocent?

When my kids were babies, I sang songs like, "Amazing Grace," "Bushel and a Peck," and of course "Jesus Loves Me" a lot. And Lord knows I prayed over my kids. I wonder what she prayed over him as she nursed. What songs did she sing? What stories did she tell? I sang songs to my kids long after they'd grown out of diapers. How long was Jochebed able to sing to Moses? Some historians say two years, others say closer to ten because often wet nurses turned into babysitters and wards of the children they were entrusted with. We can't know for sure how long she had but we can be sure that her love spoke louder than the palace's policies because he grew to know who he was deep down.

Every day, we get the choice to just float through the things we think are mundane when, in actuality, the moments matter. We must live with the intentionality that the moments we have add up, and we may never fully be able to see this side of heaven how much that privilege truly matters. One day, we will have to let our children go. No matter the length of time, what is the depth? Some of you may be watching your children walking in their Egypt enslavement or privilege and you feel like they have forgotten who they are.

Keep praying. Keep pressing. Keep loving. Keep believing that what you spoke over and into their lives will be birthed when they face hard things. You may have heard the saying "What's down in the well comes up in the bucket." Sometimes the moments we have to dig the deepest are the very moments we begin to remember who we truly are.

"Remember who you are *and...*" is a phrase I would always say to my boys anytime they were about to leave the house. I would hold them hostage with my stares until they finished the phrase "and whose you are." Often complete with eye rolls or words under their breath but never doubting (hopefully) the heart behind the mama uttering the words. I had a desperate desire for them to enter the world knowing they represented their last name well (the Schaers), but also for them to remember above all else whose they were (The Lord's). I so fervently wanted *them* to remember that somehow *I* forgot my kids were really God's. I realize now that I wanted the "Lord's best" *if it meant they were still under my roof.* I never once considered the Lord was asking me to remember whose they were with the premise that He had the authority to call one home.

Moses lived in what literature experts call "double consciousness." He was of Hebrew descent living among the Egyptian royalty, which made his own identity and loyalties difficult. He didn't have cultural authority in either group of people, but God had given him a passion for protecting others and seeking justice. That led to killing an Egyptian who was harming a Hebrew (Exodus 2:11), intervening between two Hebrews arguing (v. 12), and—after Pharaoh found out and ordered his death—fleeing to Midian, where he came to the rescue of women in the rural area:

> *Now a priest of Midian had seven daughters, and they came to draw water and fill the troughs to water their father's flock. Some shepherds came along and drove them away, but Moses got up and came to their rescue and watered their flock.*
>
> *When the girls returned to Reuel their father, he asked them, "Why have you returned so early today?"*
>
> *They answered, "An Egyptian rescued us from the shepherds. He even drew water for us and watered the flock." "And where is he?" Reuel asked his daughters. "Why did you leave him? Invite him to have something to eat."*

(Exodus 2:11-20)

Running from an adopted title and his people, Moses likely felt like a fraud and an outcast. This scene reminds me of the movie *The Lion King* just a bit—maybe it's just me. I know the storyline is a bit different from Moses, but similarly in defending his father's people, he takes the matter too far and ends up on the run, where he tries to pretend that nothing ever happened. While hiding out at a well after a long journey through the desert, he defends his new found friends (for Moses, the daughters of Reul rather than Timon and Pumbaa) and ends up with a wife. (Queue up Elton John's "Can You Feel the Love Tonight?") Far away from the confines of the palace and the watchful eye of both Pharaoh and discriminating fellow Hebrews, Moses settles into his mundane desert season.

Not a lot is written about this season. Not a lot is written because there probably wasn't much to write. He's herding sheep. He's tending the land. He's becoming a father and serving his father-in-law. Moses' first desert season lasted longer than Jesus even walked this earth. Forty years. The parallel of the forty years Moses spent in the desert compared to the forty days Jesus spent in the desert is no mistake. Forty in the Bible symbolizes new life and new growth. God wasn't doing nothing during Moses' desert season. It took God forty years of burning away old patterns and creating something new in the depths of Moses' soul before God knew he could be trusted with a burning bush. Which is the greater miracle? The bush that won't burn or the stripping away of man-made palaces and self-appointed identities?

Our desert seasons have purpose. Don't grow weary with ordinary things like feeding sheep (or children), tending to land (or your home), or working for another man (or marketplace). You may feel unseen, but one of the most extraordinary things about this life *are* the ordinary things of this life. We won't all be called out of the desert to lead multitudes, but we will all leave footprints of impact. We will all have desert seasons. The question is will we leave it the same as we went into it?

Neurosurgeon Dr. Lee Warren in his book *Hope Is the First Dose,* writes, "You can't wait for the pain to go away before you start moving, because it never goes away. Every day you don't move, the pain will just get worse, and you'll eventually prove yourself right that it's hopeless."

When I was about twelve years old, I began to notice a bulging lump on my knee. I had pointed it out to my mom, and as any good mom in the late eighties and early nineties did, she took a quick glance and said, "Hmmm, I don't see anything. Looks fine to me." I shrugged it off and went about my day. A few weeks later, playing softball, as I rounded first base and prepared to slide into second, I heard a loud pop. One of my tendons had caught on something and caused an immense amount of pain. We soon found out that I had a strangely formed calcium deposit in the form of a hook (or bone spur) that didn't want to share any room with my tendons.

After surgery and twelve weeks of recovery, I soon learned that the pain I had gone through up until that point was nothing compared to what I was about to experience: physical therapy. They had me bending my knee in ways I'm not sure I could have moved *before* the surgery and pushing myself through the pain in order to recover. One thing the physical therapists kept saying over and over again was, "You have to move in order to heal." Dr. Warren so eloquently points out that our heart and our hope are very similar.

We have to keep moving regardless of the pain. The only way to actually heal is to use the very muscles that hurt. Staying still causes us to become rigid and unable to move. When we walk through really hard things and desert seasons, the very thing we often want to do is stop moving.

Being stuck in a desert season doesn't mean you *stop*. You keep taking another step and another and another until one day, you realize you were moving toward something. I don't believe Moses was out looking for a burning bush when he stumbled on it. He was doing what he could: tending to the needs of his family and his soul.

Some days, tending to my family and my soul is just mustering up the energy to make my bed. Today, I'm typing these words to you, and that is my best yes. Tomorrow, I may literally add things to a to-do list just to feel like I've accomplished something. That's okay! My every right yes (be it little or big) is a step at moving forward and that counts for something.

"Don't despise these small beginnings." (Zechariah 4:10)

What are you tending to today?

Just because we don't have the strength today doesn't mean we won't ever have strength. And God will pull us out of bed when it's time for us to tend to even more. Those small beginnings build toward more, and God has plans for it. While Moses may have preferred to keep tending to his family and soul long after he recovered from his messy upbringing and crime, God appeared to him. If his objections were any indication, he was not interested in something requiring more. "Who am I? What would I say? Why me? I've gone through enough God! Pick someone else!"

Those are the phrases God tends to hear from me when I'm asked to do anything outside my comfort zone and let me tell you, I am a *huge* fan of my comfort zone. It's cozy there. I love it there, and I usually like it there alone. If I'm honest, as a self-described introvert, the desert doesn't really sound all that bad. In fact, what I'm realizing now even more than ever is that I would often rather take up shop and pitch a tent in the desert than fight my way out. Sure it may be hot and sandy, filled with salty tears, but it doesn't require much. As I read the words of Moses, I have a feeling he felt that same way.

> *But Moses said to God, "Who am I that I should go to Pharaoh and bring the Israelites out of Egypt?"*
>
> (Exodus 3:11)
>
> *"What if they do not believe me or listen to me and say, 'The LORD did not appear to you'?"*
>
> (Exodus 4:1)
>
> *Moses said to the LORD, "Pardon your servant, Lord. I have never been eloquent, neither in the past nor since you have spoken to your servant. I am slow of speech and tongue."*
>
> (Exodus 4:10)
>
> *But Moses said, "Pardon your servant, Lord. Please send someone else."*
>
> (Exodus 4:13)

Just because we are called to something does not mean that it will be without fear and trembling. Moses approaches the burning bush not like some gallant superhero but as a stuttering shepherd feeling unqualified. He begs God to choose someone else. He has lived through a lot already. It was cozy and comfortable tending sheep.

Three weeks before we lost our son, my husband and I had just left the comforts of our home church with a consistent salary and nice title to go with it. "Pastor's wife." It's almost laughable now to think about it, but I remember having a good pity party on the phone with my friend Mollie. She and her husband have been there through every ministry season of ours (the good and the bad), and I was complaining about the fact that I knew God was calling us to a new one. I literally used the phrase with her, "We have had so many seasons of living on manna (like the bread in the desert God provided for the Israelites). I don't want to go back to it. I know He will provide if we step out, but we are so comfortable right now."

He had birthed in our hearts a new ministry and we had just taken the leap to start building "Broken for Better." With years of marriage coaching and our own miraculous story of a redeemed marriage, we felt excited to step into a new season of helping others find purpose and hope in their families and marriages. Little did we know our marriage was about to face what would be the biggest and darkest battle, the loss of a child.

To say we were thrown into a desert is a gross understatement, so I understand if you (like me) find comfort there. We have asked God the hard questions, the Moses questions. *Why me? Who would listen? Why would my voice matter? Do you see me here in the desert? I've lost my voice! Please, God, send someone else.*

I've often wondered why God chose certain people, and Moses is no exception. Growing up, I was always taught because God wanted the glory, He always chose the "least of these" and maybe that is partly true, but I tend to believe that if God is good and gracious and better than any earthly father, He would have never seen Moses as less than and doesn't need to choose the poor and lowly to build his own resume. No, He wouldn't have been angry with Moses not wanting to face his Egypt. He would have wanted him to see how valuable he was, and that Egypt had no authority over him.

My God would have known that the boy who donned the walls of a palace but didn't let the palace change him, needed to be reminded of the real Kingdom that ran through his veins. The Kingdom of God. Whatever good or bad Moses faced while being an adopted prince of Egypt, God was going to redeem and use it for good. Our past traumas, when faced with heaven in mind, will do more than just set ourselves free; it can free multitudes.

We can either heal and help others, or we can hide and run. We either pound our chests at the enemy and continue to stoop low to wash feet or pound our chests at God and attempt to find comfort in the desert. To be clear, I have done both. Some things will happen in this life that we cannot see coming. Some things you don't prepare for, but no matter what, no matter the circumstances, who you are will be multiplied in the trials. Chris Voss says in his book *Never Split the Difference*, "When the pressure is on, you don't rise to the occasion. You fall to your highest level of preparation."

Sometimes I feel disqualified. Disqualified because as a mom who lost a son, I feel I may never smile again, love again, find joy again, and love others with that deep unadulterated love again. That's the funny thing about light versus dark. The dark wants to so brazenly invade the light that it tries to convince you not just that you will not make it, but that you aren't even *worthy* to make it out:

You couldn't stop that horrific thing that happened, so you don't deserve to. You couldn't stop the death, the divorce, the sickness, or the heartache, so this is who you are now. Hiding in the shadows, hiding in your desert. Peeking out at glimpses of everyone else's sunlight or social media highlight longing for a little warmth from it. Scared that others will point and find pity at you trying on that uncomfortable smile or even wonder how you dare have the audacity to step out of the shadows.

Friend. If you find yourself there, as I have, I'm humbly offering you my little nudge. Step out. You'll be okay. You may run back to the shadows from time to time, but people need you out here. Maybe not the people you expected, but there are others. Others who will cheer you on. Others who wear new lenses of loss too. Others, like us, who used to think those shade glasses were meant to remind you of the shadows but in actuality, they just help you see others differently.

Our stories (and our hurts) matter, and our hard things can either drive us or crush us—and sometimes both at the same time. Don't be scared to take a step closer to that burning bush. The one who is calling out who you truly are. He knows our struggles, our trauma, and our pain. He isn't taken back by it or bothered by it. He knows our stories from beginning to end and isn't calling us out to "use" us but to redeem us and our stories.

> *"You intended to harm me, but God intended it for good to accomplish what is now being done, the saving of many lives."*

(Genesis 5:20)

Step out of the desert one step at a time. There are others who need our stuttering stories and weary hearts. Confront our Egypt and embrace God's best.

Chapter 9

Bragging Rights

It was the second Christmas without our youngest. We got through it a little easier than the first year, but there is never anything normal about making new memories and knowing there is someone missing. Crazy enough, the year before God welcomed him home, we had decided as a family to set a new precedent regarding Christmas gifts and what the future would look like as we celebrated. Knowing Santa makes toys and not lawn mowers or TVs, Amazon wish lists with young-adult-size dreams were starting to rob the joy just a tad as we struggled to make the most of a very limited budget. (I'm sure you can relate.)

We were starting to realize those fun family traditions and Christmas magic we loved so much as the kids were little got a whole lot harder as we became bird launchers (a term my friend Tracy chooses to use instead of empty-nesters, and I think I've adopted it.) In lieu of gifts, as a family, we decided to each year pick a new place or thing to do together. Oh, how thankful I am now God laid that on our hearts before tragedy struck. It truly helped us that first Christmas navigate what felt like a windstorm of failed expectations, emotions, and heartache. We had something to look forward to, and that was time together.

This Christmas just like the last, we planned a little trip for the kids, and they in turn gave us an amazing gift: a nice dinner out. The date came for us to all get dressed up and hit the town. Just as we were about to hop in the car, my middle son took a call from his wife saying she would try her best to make it, but she was needing to help her parents with car trouble. He seemed flustered but determined not to let it change the plans. My other daughter-in-law said, "You and Kurt go with the boys so you don't miss the reservation, and I'll go swing by and pick her up since they need the car and meet you there."

It wasn't the plan as expected, but we were going to make the most of it. The boys were excited about the destination they had kept secret and guaranteed we had never been to this award-winning restaurant before. Once in the car, they said, "Okay, you have to keep your eyes closed until we get there."

At first, we thought they were joking, but they were very adamant, so of course we played along. I kid you not, those kids drove us around for nearly an hour. Interstate, left turn, right turn…wait, are we back on the interstate again? For a solid fifteen minutes, I thought for sure I knew right where we were, but after so many stops and starts and turning this way and that, I honestly had no idea which direction we were headed. Through my shut eyelids, I would get glimmers of light every now and then, and a smell or noise of some certain part of town, but after a while, all my senses were against me, and I can say I was truly lost. Once we arrived, they helped us out of the car and allowed us to open our eyes to reveal our destination was…home. They had driven us in circles just long enough for the girls to prepare an unbelievable candle-lit dinner complete with four courses and even entertainment. Laughter and happy tears fell hard as we all ate together, and it was a night we will never forget.

The very next day, Kurt and I found ourselves in the front row at church lost in worship. As I closed my eyes and prayed, I pictured my son next to the throne room. Tears once again streamed down my cheeks.

My eyes were closed just like they were on that car ride the night before, and the realization washed over me that I felt the exact same as I had the night before. Lost. Glimmers of hope would stir as I saw the light bounce between the tears and my fluttering eyelids, but I knew, even as I have so painstakingly tried my best to write words to encourage your heart and hopefully mine, I have been walking with God this last year and half with my eyes closed, wondering which way was next and where we would end up. Sometimes when God gives us dreams, we expect the experience to be easy. We expect life to resemble a good navigation app with warnings up ahead and with the destination and timeline clear. Feeling lost along the way is never part of the plan, and we surely don't ever expect to end up right back where we started.

No one knows a winding, almost circular map better than Joseph. Much of his journey was spent with his eyes closed—in prayer, in despair, and most often, in dreams.

Have you ever had a dream, and no one believed in it but you? Or better yet, you shared it with the wrong person (or maybe prematurely) and were met with doubt or judgment? No matter the dream, it will take work to accomplish it. Be careful not to expose a dream meant for you to a world that isn't for you.

At just seventeen years old, the "favored" one we're here to study is Joseph. The dreamer. Filled with God-sized dreams and no one who believed them, Joseph in obedience to his father heads out to meet his brothers and is met with the first big roadblock: sibling rivalry in its grandest form, hate. He had dreams of eleven bundles of grain (the exact same number of brothers he was telling) bowing down to his bundle. Then another dream of the eleven stars and the sun and the moon (representing his parents and his brothers) bowing down to him.

After they had already seen their father play favorites by giving him a fresh new trendy fit and *nada* for them, they weren't too thrilled by what seemed to be a not-so-humble brag. Surely Joseph had a lot to learn when it came to humility and reading the room, but at just seventeen years old, he must have thought that the world was for him and those closest to him would be his biggest cheerleaders.

> *So Joseph went after his brothers and found them near Dothan. But they saw him in the distance, and before he reached them, they plotted to kill him.*
>
> *"Here comes that dreamer!" they said to each other. "Come now, let's kill him and throw him into one of these cisterns and say that a ferocious animal devoured him. Then we'll see what comes of his dreams."*
>
> *When Reuben heard this, he tried to get rescue him from their hands. "Let's not take his life," he said. "Don't shed any blood. Throw him into this cistern here in the wilderness, but don't lay a hand on him." Reuben said this to rescue him from them and take him back to his father.*
>
> *So when Joseph came to his brothers, they stripped him of his robe—the ornate robe he was wearing—and they took him and threw him into the cistern. The cistern was empty; there was no water in it.*

(Genesis 37:18-24)

Stripped of his robe, they were taking more than just a prized possession. They were trying to replace his identity. Favored? A leader? I can hear them now. "Who do you think you are? You will lead us? You are a prideful, arrogant daddy's boy. Where is he to protect you now?" Surely Joseph was learning a life lesson, but he was learning even more than that. You don't share dreams with those who don't dream. You also don't share them with those that want to always keep you beneath them.

In a house raising three boys, there were many times sibling rivalry was elevated, feelings hurt, or competitive spirits heated. We tried often and hard to pull out the leadership and dreams we saw in each of our boys and challenged them to call it out in each other. I know we weren't perfect by any means, but I have deep fond memories (and pictures to prove it) of each boy excelling at some dream of choice, be it a sport or performance or victory, and them hoisting the other up or dog-piling the victor like you see on a baseball diamond after a World Series win or the football field after a Super Bowl. We need to pick wisely who we let into our dreams, deepest revelations, or victories. Not everyone around us is ready to hoist us up and celebrate with us. If and when that is the case, we need to be protective over our dreams and hold onto them until God has had time to work them out in us.

Reading Joseph sharing his dreams with his brothers after knowing how it goes, I often cringe. Why couldn't he have kept them to himself? His brothers conspired against him, eventually selling him for twenty shekels (a kind of silver worth about $200). They watched him get carried off to Egypt. Reuben had begged his brothers not to kill Joseph, but he wasn't prepared for the second plot in motion while he had been tending to the flock.

When Reuben returned to the cistern and saw that Joseph was not there, he tore his clothes. He went back to his brothers and said, "The boy isn't there! Where can I turn now?"

To cover their tracks and provide answers for their father, they dipped his beautiful robe in goat blood and asked his father to confirm if it was Joseph's.

He recognized it and said, "It is my son's robe! Some ferocious animal has devoured him. Joseph has surely been torn to pieces." Then Jacob tore his clothes, put on sackcloth and mourned for his son many days. All his sons and daughters came to comfort him, but he refused to be comforted. "No," he said, "I will continue to mourn until I join my son in the grave." So his father wept for him.

(Genesis 37:28-34)

My heart hurts for Joseph's father as I read these verses. I can literally feel the pain in my chest as I hear those words knowing what he felt in those moments. It's heavier still when we remember in most losses, we never know the full story or the reason why. No matter what loss we walk through, crying out to God, "Why?" is often an answer we may never get.

Did he see how unhealthy his family had gotten? Did he see how much the favoritism he showed was tearing his family apart? He is told a lie to cover up the real cause of his loss, not knowing that the way he was leading his family was at the root of it, but would he have drastically changed his ways if he knew the atmosphere of favoritism he bred in his home would lead to this? His own life as a boy had been one nurtured with slander and family issues as he cheated his own brother Esau out of a birthright with the help of his mother's favoritism, but here, history repeats itself and more hurt is the outcome. Healing our own past generational trauma is so important. We may think we have moved on and are no longer affected by things in our past, but if we aren't careful to allow God to expose hurtful patterns and wounded parts of our heart, we will repeat the very same issues and project them onto our children.

Jacob in this moment declares he will continue to mourn until he joins his son in the grave, and part of me understands that to my core.

When you lose someone, there will always be a part of you that mourns and grieves what was lost. Always. There is no easy way around it or quick fix to the pain. You will forever walk differently, but there is a difference between learning to walk with your grief or deciding to sit down in it. Learning to move in spite of your trauma, walking shakily beside your unmet expectations and the life you now face, you will either learn to hold both tenderly at the very same time, or you will wreck the other amazing relationships around you and do more than just experience grief.

You will become it.

My family and I navigated grief like Jacob's together in the January(s) after losing our beloved Logan. Sure, we'd had a few months to scream and cry, but grief is not a timed prognosis. We were not ready for the messages of the New Year, but the bread and butter of any good start-of-the-year sermon, social media campaign, and radio televangelism is the "name it and claim it," moving-on kind of hope. The audio sound bites of the churches that were filling my social media feeds were declaring series titles with words like "More" and "Overflow" and "Abundance."

Those words are powerful and needed and true, but what happens when you stumble into church longing for hope, are met with promises of more, but still find yourself in a pit of despair? What do those words mean when you are walking so close to God you're bumping feet, yet still experience more heartache than victory? Do those words ring true when you are walking in favor with God but suffering? We felt like the Christian community of "more" and "abundance" put expectations on us to push through, start fresh, and make sure we're wearing rose-colored glasses regardless of what our lives and our hearts are enduring—as though perhaps our grief is our own doing. As though God's vision and character changes based on what we do (or don't do).

Joseph's "more" and "abundance" probably felt sarcastic as he wiped floors, doted on Potifer, and swatted away advances from his master's wife. It's hard to pursue God's dreams in survival mode, but that's precisely how God fulfilled them. His strength to keep taking the next right step was possible because he was in a position that required it.

Alicia Britt Chole says in her book *The Night Is Normal*, "…we continue to expect a Garden of Eden faith in a Garden of Gethsemane age." (Paradise itself and the garden where Jesus prayed to the Father not to crucify him). We must be careful that when preaching on faith, we aren't teaching that our current outcomes are solely dependent on our perfection, or that the goodness of God is dependent on our happy family or bank account. You can be blessed and still have trials. You can have favor and still have people come against you and challenge your character. You can be walking with God and still have things, titles, positions, and purpose ripped from your hands. You can run naked as a jay bird away from sin and can still be accused.

As Joseph enters his next "favored" position with the grand title of slave, the scripture says the Lord was with Joseph, and his master saw it. Everything the master owned, he put in the hands of Joseph. Potiphar (the master) didn't concern himself with anything except the food he put in his belly because he trusted Joseph to handle everything else. He knew anything that boy touched would be well because God was with him.

What the enemy tried to continually take from Joseph (his identity and his character), God was using as a building block to fulfill a dream. I believe in this second roadblock of being falsely accused, God was using what was meant to harm Joseph as a way out of a palace that could have kept him comfortable in order to pave the way into a palace that would influence eternity—saving more than his own soul but a nation with the wisdom God was about to give him.

One day he went into the house to attend to his duties, and none of the household servants was inside. She caught him by his cloak and said, "Come to bed with me!" But he left his cloak in her hand and ran out of the house.

When she saw that he had left his cloak in her hand and had run out of the house, she called her household servants. "Look," she said to them, "this Hebrew has been brought to us to make sport of us! He came in here to sleep with me, but I screamed. When he heard me scream for help, he left his cloak beside me and ran out of the house."

She kept his cloak beside her until his master came home. Then she told him this story: "That Hebrew slave you brought us came to me to make sport of me. But as soon as I screamed for help, he left his cloak beside me and ran out of the house."

When his master heard the story his wife told him, saying, "This is how your slave treated me," he burned with anger. Joseph's master took him and put him in prison, the place where the king's prisoners were confined.

(Genesis 39:11-20)

You may be lied about and thrown into a prison (of mind or reality), but you are not alone. In order to make it in a world that grows darker and darker and will continue as we draw closer to our King's return, we need to realize that the day we are walking in has purpose whether we are in a pit, a prison, or a palace. Your current situation or location does not prove or discredit God's hand on your life. Man may see no value in you, but the enemy does, and he wants you to believe that every heartache is proof God doesn't care. The enemy doesn't care if your address is 7309 Pharoah Drive or inmate number #2340983. The only thing the enemy wants is for you to doubt God sees you right where you are.

The first time I went to prison was about five years ago. Inmate #2340983 is actually my number. In prison, no matter what you are there for, everyone is given one because your identity has nothing to do with who you are, where you came from, or where you are headed. You are just a number. Now although you won't find me on an episode of *Pastor's Wives Gone Wild* or the *Real Housewives of Wesley Chapel*, that number is actually mine. When you serve time in prison, be it for a crime or to help those in the prison, you get a number. Thankfully my story (at least for now) is crime free, and I got mine in order to be allowed in. The process of getting a prison number is quite an undertaking in the state of Florida. Background checks and fingerprints along with every detail of my sorted life were needed. I understand why, but it is kind of comical to think about how hard of a process it is to get into a prison when everyone there is desperately wanting out.

When you walk through those metal detectors and are searched by hand before the first barbed wire gate slams shut behind you and they hand you a panic button in case anything goes wrong, the last thing you are thinking is, "Man, I bet there are some amazing women in this place." The destination and location immediately avail yourself to think there is *no way* God could be moving in a place like this, and in no way could He have His hand on the hearts in here.

What I met in that little chapel we held worship services in was the exact opposite. We got to witness a woman get her Biblical Doctorate degree and leave ready to serve others in her own community with the knowledge of being behind bars, ready to war hell to help others not choose the same life. We got to see nightclub singers turned into worship leaders, with songs written in their jail cells strummed beautifully on the old, donated chapel guitar in front of their cell mates. We got to see young women who had just arrived scared to death meet God for the very first time. We also got to pray over women who were up for parole but were so scared to leave. Prison had proved safer for them than the homes they came from. I have so many more stories I wish I could share, but the point is favor can be found anywhere. The women I met in that prison worshiped more freely than any pastor or prophet I have ever met (and I mean that truly). I guess Jesus knew what he was saying when he shared the parable of the one forgiven that owed the larger debt (Luke 7:36-50).

> *Neither of them had the money to pay him back, so he forgave the debts of both. Now which of them will love him more?" Simon replied, "I suppose the one who had the bigger debt forgiven." "You have judged correctly," Jesus said.*

Hope is not handcuffed to our location or circumstances.

Joseph was favored as a slave because he was an honest and hard worker. He was favored as a prisoner because he was trustworthy. Blessings and favor are not a position of destination; they are a position of the heart, and Joseph was determined to make the position of his heart one that served the true purpose he was created for: his eternal King.

Joseph's posture in all his situations mattered, and so does ours. How we fare behind bars, in our unseen moments, is noticed by God. If we cling to Him in times of pits and prisons only as a means to escape, we're not displaying our potential to strengthen His Kingdom. You have to know who the King is on the inside of you to walk with the same stature and grace in a prison as you do into a palace. Neither one is a "'greater" calling. God can use the same person to highlight what He needs in any environment because He knows the person He trusts is the same no matter where they are.

> When Joseph came to them the next morning, he saw that they were dejected. So he asked Pharaoh's officials who were in custody with him in his master's house, "Why do you look so sad today?"
>
> "We both had dreams," they answered, "but there is no one to interpret them."
>
> Then Joseph said to them, "Do not interpretations belong to God? Tell me your dreams."

(Genesis 40:6-8)

Joseph *saw* that they were dejected. He asked why they looked sad. Here we find our dreamer not in a modern prison but an ancient prison that I'm sure lacked a balanced meal, a nice chapel, and decent plumbing. He could have kept to himself and cared less about those in his presence, but we see him looking at the hearts of others. God gives us all discernment if we ask for it, but we have the ability to walk right past someone's pain because of our own trials if we aren't careful. We may miss something huge when we are so focused on ourselves and where we thought we would be or what we thought life would look like that we don't extend love to those in the same place as us. Supporting someone stuck in their own prison may potentially allow them to see they are not alone *and* give you purpose and freedom in yours. Don't miss this.

After Joseph interprets the dreams of the cupbearer and the baker and both come to fruition, he asks the one that is reinstated to the palace to remember him.

> *"Remember me and show me kindness; mention me to Pharaoh and get me out of this prison."*

(Genesis 40:14)

One of the very hardest things I have had to try to process this last year and half on top of the loss of my son is the loss of people. So many don't know how to handle grief or are so concerned they may say or do the wrong thing, so they just decide to do nothing at all. People that we truly felt close to up until the time of the accident dropped off the face of the earth. Those we had helped in the dark of night. Those caught in their own prisons or heartaches. Those we rallied behind and championed on platforms and behind closed doors seemed to disappear as if they never knew us.

Grief has a way of multiplying itself, and every loss can feel deeper and bigger as you walk through the process of healing such raw and real unknown parts of your heart. I am sure as Joseph sat waiting for a hopeful call from the palace those first few days or weeks he felt much the same way. "Did you forget me? Did you forget how I ministered to your heart? Did how I care for you even matter?"

People will let us down. Even God's people will let us down (don't forget the very brothers that threw him into the pit would one day represent the twelve tribes of Israel). Do your best to not be focused on the ones who aren't there for you and be thankful for the few that are. You will not be able to bring everyone where God is taking you. We don't need to remind others of our gifts, talents or character in order to be used by God. He will expose and call on us in His time, whether others recognize it or not. We aren't walking through our life's desert or prison seasons for anyone's calling other than our own.

Joseph spends two more years unseen, serving time in a prison for a crime he did not commit. How does he keep bitterness from taking root in every cell of his body while he tends the cells of criminals? Eventually, Joseph is remembered, and Pharaoh summons him immediately. As Joseph interprets the dream of the troubled Pharaoh and gives him the foresight of the coming plague, he gives *no* credence to his own skill but all to God. He knows that this gift is not his own. He knows that no one will directly bow to him but should only bow to God and soon, he will see that many will bow to the God living inside of him.

Do you see the shift? What he boasted about to his brothers all those years ago had little if anything to do with him. It all had to do with the position of his heart and the God who ruled it. It may not be a mighty man or woman of God that comes looking for, believing in, or needing the God-sized dream inside of you. It may very well be a Pharaoh, a godless leader, or a generation that sees all you have been through and needs the spirit living inside of you. Your family may disown you and see no value in you. Your employer may cast you off and replace you with someone less qualified (like Potiphar). You may be stuck in a prison of mundane tasks just waiting on someone to take notice with hands in fists to a God that gave you a dream thrust in the stars.

We can get so caught up in the dreams we never saw fulfilled that we become the very reason He can never fulfill them. From the age of seventeen to the age of thirty, Joseph waited to see his dreams fulfilled.

As Joseph gathered the crops for the seven years of abundance as the

Pharaoh's right-hand man and prepared for the famine, he was given the king's daughter's hand in marriage and starts a family. What he names his children is very interesting.

If someone tells you to not think of the word "elephant," what are you going to think of? An elephant, right? And yet here we find him declaring with names that will be his children's forever! Manasseh and Ephraim.

> *Joseph named his firstborn Manasseh and said, "It is because God has made me forget all my trouble and all my father's household."*

(Genesis 41:51)

"I'm going to name you something I no longer want to think about! Gone are my family and gone are my troubles."

There are some things, just like the loss of a child, that no matter how hard and how far we run from it, they will *always* go with us and be part of our story. We can try to run from our past trauma or say it doesn't matter, but our past is in part what made us. We can't outrun the very thing that created who we became.

Ephraim was named so because God made Joseph *"fruitful in the land of his suffering"* (v. 52). He wasn't talking about the famine here because he would have had plenty in his position, and his son was born before the famine had even hit. He was talking about the suffering he had endured up to this point. He was declaring with faith that even though he had lost all connection with his bloodline and the father that loved him so well, he was choosing joy. Choosing to look at the fruit and realizing his hurdles brought him to where he was, he would not let it hold him back. The spiritual "famines" we walk through when walked out in faith have the ability to lead generations.

The dreams God gave us don't need our striving and our planning to come to pass. He only needs a pure heart.

Genesis 41:9 says after Joseph sees his brother's bow down, *"Then, he remembered his dreams about them."* He wasn't walking around thinking about failed dreams, shaking his fists at God and consumed that maybe God had gotten it wrong. He was doing his best to live a faith-filled life, taking one right step at a time when, **BAM**! He is reminded and immediately sees his dream become a reality. Joseph, after seeing his brothers, realizing his dreams have all come true, is immediately faced with the family he has so recently declared he would forget about and longs to meet his new brother and see his aging father. I wish when it came to walking with hope during chaos, I could say "like father like son," but unfortunately it appears that Jacob, unlike Joseph, was truly struggling to walk well while carrying grief.

Please hear me. I don't blame him for it. He believed those dreams his favored son had shared with him went to the grave. He was overcome by the loss, but twenty years later, Jacob is still overcome by it and has lost hope. As his boys journey back to him with one brother staying behind under custody and now with the assignment to bring Joseph's little brother to Egypt in hopes for food to save the family, we find Jacob's response…

> *"You have deprived me of my children. Joseph is no more and Simeon is no more, and now you want to take Benjamin. Everything is against me!"*
>
> *Then Reuben said to his father, "You may put both of my sons to death if I do not bring him back to you. Entrust him to my care, and I will bring him back."*

But Jacob said, "My son will not go down there with you; his brother is dead and he is the only one left. If harm comes to him on the journey you are taking, you will bring my gray head down to the grave in sorrow."

(Genesis 42:36-38)

Jacob was so fearful to let another (favored) son go that he was almost willing to allow his entire family to starve. When facing grief, and unfortunately I know this all too well, we get so focused on the person or the thing we lost, we can forget to love the ones we have. We *must* realize there is hope found here, even as we wait for heaven. Eternity starts now. We may not be able to see our loved ones behind the veil of heaven, but that does not mean they aren't alive and well. Don't focus so much on heaven that you miss where your feet are planted. Grief has a way of letting you look right past the blessings in front of you as you long for something out of your reach.

Jacob expected the worst before it even happened. His trust in God and His protection had been shaken—and rightfully so. He didn't know his son was alive and well in some far-off land, beckoning him to come to a new home and reunite with him. He didn't trust that God was still fulfilling promises given in dreams twenty years ago. My heart aches, wishing the same were true about my son. But in reality, my story is more similar than it feels. I will see him soon. I don't know the time or date (be it twenty years or more or less), but he is thriving in a far-off land. He is happy and whole, and I believe he is cheering his family on. I can't wait until the day we are all reunited. I am just trying my best to unclench my fists (like Jacob), trusting God with my sons and my own family I still have here with me in the desert while I wait for the reunion.

So friend, which will it be? Will we choose to live like Jacob or

Joseph? Will we forgive others (or even ourselves) with the things we can't control? Joseph, as a favored one, walked through a life of heartache but was resolute to make it count and make it matter, no matter what his location or destination. He didn't wait for everything to come together and be perfect to see people where they were at. He didn't wait until his family was whole to step into his calling. He was busy taking one right step after another, and his family was saved because of it. Don't get distracted with what God has not done in your family yet. Keep taking the right steps and one day, I pray just like Joseph, you may be the very one to offer them hope and be surprised by the dreams you quickly realized have come to pass. Our endgame should never be a perfectly happy and safe life here on this revolving rock. Our destination is bigger than that. Our goal is home reunited and all together.

A Mother's Prayer

Lord, help us.

Help us unclench our fists.

Help us walk steadily through life's heartaches remembering Your promises and the dreams You've birthed in us that we have still yet to see.

Help us fight hell to keep focused on the things that matter in the light of eternity instead of our troubles of today.

And as always, Lord, give my boy a hug from me. I can't wait to wrap my arms around his neck and Yours. I know You will love him well until (and even after) I get to. I really am trying my best to make it count here on earth. Please give us all the strength to make heaven look different because of our stories here on earth.

I love You forever. I like You for always.

Mom

Epilogue

During the darkest days, God so tenderly led me to many others who have stories much the same as mine. Reading became my safe place and my solace. Soaking in other's tender words who have faced so much loss before me truly helped steady my soul and remind me to keep pressing. As I got to the end of each book, I desperately looked for another and another so that I could have something in my hands to keep reminding my soul that I wasn't alone. I wanted to leave you with some helpful resources that I have poured over, marked up with notes and pens (but more so my tears). I do so in hopes that if you find yourself at the end of this book and in more need of hope and encouragement from others who are fighting hell to keep strong and steadfast, you have some recommendations.

Whether you are disillusioned in your faith, walking through grief, or just needing hope, I pray this list helps meet you where you are. Thank you for being patient with me as I have tried my best to be true to where God has me in this journey of loss and for allowing me to share it with you. I hope to see your stories as well, as you continue to keep taking the next right step, living with heaven in mind. Let's *Make It Count*.

#MakeItCount became the mantra of our family. On my personal social media platforms, you will see a video of my son's celebration of life service that explains the heart behind it a little more and the heart's cry of a mama that was birthed in the dark of night. As a way to honor our son and the future he had planned in front of him, we started the Make It Count Scholarship Fund in order to help students with similar dreams and aspirations. If you would like more information regarding this movement, our family story, or would like to give towards helping students step into their calling, we welcome you to check out more of our story at:

https://brokenforbetter.com/make-it-count/.

Resources

Through the Eyes of a Lion – Levi Lusko[1]

Suffer Strong – Katherine and Jay Wolf

Anonymous – Alicia Britt Chole

All In – Mark Batterson[2]

Heaven Revealed – Paul Enns

Heaven – Randy Acorn

I Wasn't Ready to Say Goodbye – Brook Noel & Pamela D. Blair, PhD

A Grief Observed – C.S. Lewis

Man's Search for Meaning – Viktor Frankl

Hope is the First Dose – Dr. Lee Warren

The Night is Normal – Alicia Britt Chole

The Fight to Flourish – Jennie Lusko

Wake Up to Wonder – Whitney Hopler

Heaven Your Real Home – Joni Eareckson Tada

Restore My Soul (A Grief Companion) – Lorraine Peterson

Suffering is Never for Nothing – Elisabeth Elliot

Even if He Doesn't – Kristen LaValley

---

1 The first book I was able to process after our loss.

2 I had just finished this book right before my son's accident.

www.ingramcontent.com/pod-product-compliance
Lightning Source LLC
Chambersburg PA
CBHW020418150626
46554CB00014B/1938